****

A COUNTRY, NOT A WAR

Vietnam Impressions

****

Harold Truman

1999

Pale Bone

Thanks to and Acknowledgements to Vietnam Handbook, Random House, International Herald-Tribune, New York Times, Rough Guides, Stanley Karnow, Neil Sheehan, Penguin-Putnam, San Diego Union-Tribune, the magazine Vietnam, Pierre Schoendoerfer, Viet Nam News, Michael Bilton, Kevin Sim, Daniel Ellsberg, Institute of International Studies, U.C. Berkeley, & especially to Bao Ninh.

Excerpts from The Sorrow of War by Bao Ninh, Copyright 1995 by Bao Ninh, are reprinted by permission of Pantheon Books, a division of Random House.
Excerpts from "China's Real Agents of Change" by T. Friedman, Copyright 1998, are reprinted by permission of the New York Times.
Excerpts from A Bright Shining Lie by Neil Sheehan, Copyright 1988 by Neil Sheehan, are reprinted by permission of Random House.
Excerpts from Four Hours In My Lai by Michael Bilton and Kevin Sim, Copyright 1992 by Michael Bilton and Kevin Sim, used by permission of Viking Penguin, a division of Penguin Putnam.
Excerpts from The Rough Guide – Vietnam, Copyright 1996 by Rough Guides, used by permission of Rough Guides, Ltd.

Library of Congress Catalog Card Number 99-60641

ISBN 0-9670176-0-2

Pale Bone Publishing
San Diego

hairyt@worldnet.att.net

INTRODUCTION

"Omnia Gallia es divise en tres partes." So is Vietnam. So is this book. There is a short first section to document a few preconceptions and learn a little about its history. Then a section on the South and a section on the North.

This is no children's book. Parental discretion advised.

It is a story of impressions, nothing more or less, of different people at different times, but often of the same place.

Regarding impressions perspective is everything.

Welcome, with bloodshot eyes, to a Vietnam you've never seen before.

Harold Truman
October, 1998

Dedicated to Mom, Dad, and Petite

TABLE OF CONTENTS

THE NORTH

PROLOGUE

"WAITING FOR THE PLANE"

Paul Theroux's advice to aspiring travel writers was to tell the reader where you came from; not set her down in a foreign airport without the benefit of context.

As for Vietnam, this was especially good advice. I was of that generation which got drafted long ago. Drafted to battle in the jungle far away. Or so we thought.

The number of soldiers who actually saw combat has been estimated at less than fifteen percent. *Would I have been a clerk-typist in Saigon were I a draftee?*

It was a question I would always ask myself. I enlisted in the U.S. Army Security Agency with a guarantee that my first tour of duty would be Europe. Once in the army, I took the language qualification test, was assigned to the NSA language school, and became an "MOS 04B."

A German linguist, supposedly. The good news was that the U.S. Army did not need a lot of those in Vietnam.

But playing it safely cost me four years of involuntary servitude. One thousand, four hundred sixty days. That was how we put it.

To an American, mere mention of the "V-Word" still produced to this day a stronger emotion than all but a few other terms in the English language, especially to those of us who were young in the 1960s. Yet most Americans have never been to Vietnam. No, but we've known people who had been there during the war. We've heard stories. Read books and seen the movies.

It was surprising to open a map and read so many familiar place names: Khe Sanh, Plei Ku, Da Nang.

Now near Millennium's turn, there was a new national slogan: *"Vietnam is a country, not a war."*

Not bad public relations. Most of the guidebooks had it on page one. A clever slogan, it made a good point. Unfortunately there were still folks around here who had yet to forget the American Civil War, and it was aeons ago.

For many Americans, Vietnam was a country, a war, and an era. Korea excepted, this distinguished it from other places on the globe.

Thirty-two years ago in 1965 during the Christmas holidays, I sat on a chair lift in Aspen, riding by myself, thinking about a certain predicament I had gotten into.

As a consequence, I assumed I would soon be "visiting a foreign country," as they put it horoscopes. Riding to the top of Buttermilk Mountain, snowflakes in my face, I pictured how different it would be. And how frightening it would be to hit the ground in Vietnam as a foreign soldier.

I supposed that almost every place in Vietnam was mined. Beneath the earth sat something that would take a leg. Or rake off your balls. Or stab a foot in filthy goo with a pointy stick, or steal your finger. Or blow off two legs, not one. Or kill you, which seemed better than losing both legs.

Although I was on "extended-extended" scholastic probation at the university, I had quit going to Spanish class in October only three weeks into the semester. I hadn't bothered to drop the course, and American Marines were about to suffer a huge loss in a place that sounded to me like somewhere east of Shangri La: The Ia Drang Valley.

I really should have seen it coming a year earlier on a night at the fraternity house just before the poker games started after dinner. President Lyndon B. Johnson was on the black-and-white

2

television, addressing us fellow Americans. As we gathered to watch, LBJ said that where *he* came from, (Texas, which was here we were), "You could tell a man by the coonskins on his wall."

LBJ dramatically whirled around to illustrate.

I squinted at the television. Sure enough, he had five or six raccoon tails temporarily tacked on the wall behind, which was somewhere in the White House.

No one at the fraternity house was sure what the hell he was talking about. Davey Crockett, perhaps?

Next, Lyndon mentioned something about the Gulf of Tonkin.

We had never heard of it, so who cared? We were anxious to drink a few brews, play a little poker, and take a wee bit more of O'Connel's money. He played every night and always lost.

Mornings, I would usually be at the student union for coffee and chocolate doughnuts. By January 1966, shortly after Aspen, I had developed a plan. It was something like: Stay flat on the ground. Burrow as far as possible. Don't shoot back.

Growing up where I did, I knew what guns could do to a person's good looks.

The day was crisp and sunny, a winter's day during Finals, when I plopped down at the union cafeteria and gaily popped open the student newspaper, anticipating nothing more than another productive morning at the Longhorn Billiard Club. Vietnam had become a hot topic. LBJ had thrown down the glove.

A small box-story on the front page was about an ambush the day before. The Viet Cong had placed a land mine on a dirt road and the lead truck in an American convoy had blown up. But that was not unusual. After all, it was the same way Dirty Don had gotten it. He was a black guy who had gone over to Vietnam and returned with a pronounced limp and a piece of shrapnel in his butt.

What was nasty about the ambush I was reading about was

what happened next: GIs cleared out of the trucks after the lead transport was blown to smithereens. They raced to the paddies at each side of the road and hit the ground beside the raised highway. But the Viet Cong wiped out all of them. The VC had set up machine guns six inches off the ground, knowing exactly where the troops would be headed. The VC had calmly waited to commence firing until the last GI bailed out of his vehicle.

My goodness, I thought.

My best-laid plans to stay alive in one piece gargled down the drain. Vietnam was out of the question. Off the drawing board.

Nix. Nein. Vorsicht!

Ten months later, I was at Fort Dix, New Jersey, where I waited for three days to catch a hop to Berlin. There were more Green Berets than I could count, hanging around, killing time with me. It was no happy place under any circumstances. They were going to the Big Bad Nam, of course. Most of them were frightened about dying. Though Green Berets, they looked miserable. I felt sorry for them.

Many were younger than I was.

And they didn't look so tough, waiting for the plane.

"THE SHADOW"

Like Martin Sheen in *Apocalypse Now*, I intended to go up the river. Not down it.

Vietnam was shaped like a serpent S. I planned to start toward the bottom, in the South, thinking it would get continuously stranger as we progressed northward.

My wife, Petite, left the country in 1967 at the age of twenty to go to school in San Mateo, California. She has been back to her homeland five times, three times since 1975 when the country was unified. She has never been north of the DMZ. Her family was originally from Hue, of the royal family. She was a relative of Bao Dai, the eighty-year-old playboy who still lived in Paris, the exiled would-be king.

Petite went to high school in Saigon. Before she left, she worked for Pan Am as a ticket agent at Tan Son Nhat, the airport where we'll land and enter the country. I'll welcome a little familiarity to start with. Even Saigon would likely be strange, and I want a retreat. A redoubt.

The Rex Hotel: Western bar. Ex-Pats. Other tourists. English Spoken Here. Pizza!

Then we shall proceed to the weird stuff.

Already I have witnessed some of the weirdness here in America; visiting Vietnamese in-laws in L.A. Never order a dish called "Duck Blood." Also, I've discovered that the Vietnamese have been placed on earth for a sacred mission.

That is, to *eat*.

They're even worse than Americans. On par with the Chinese and French. Don't let those slender bodies fool you. Food seemed like it was a national obsession to me, at least among the South Vietnamese.

"Food. Glorious Food!"

From *Oliver*, that was a song Petite often chirped in our kitchen.

However, I did plan to drink a glass of snake blood over there, duly recorded with color photographs. A macho thing, of course, and I planned to take advantage of the firing range at the Cu Chi tunnels and fire an AK-47 rifle.

In Hue, I intended to go off the beaten track up to the former Demilitarized Zone on the sixteenth parallel. Have the driver creep up Highway 9 into no man's land, the jungles and mountains. Stop by Khe Sanh firebase. Cross the Ho Chi Minh Trail. Peek at the border with Laos.

At least one day upriver, somewhere near the "heart of darkness," looking for the shadow of Kurtz.

"HISTORY WEIGHS HEAVILY"

"For most Westerners, Vietnam is synonymous with a jungle war that pitted the greatest power on earth against a mysterious country in the East."

That was the opening sentence from **Vietnam Handbook**. It went on to say that most Vietnamese were now too young to remember the war.

The opening sentence from the **Rough Guide** was: *"History weighs heavily on **Vietnam**."*

Most Westerners had trouble with Vietnamese names. It was a tonal language; the names difficult to remember, to pronounce, and to differentiate. Also, Vietnam's history had been independent of American history until about the past fifty years. Therefore, the subject of little interest in the United States.

Recorded Vietnamese history began in the second century BC when the Chinese moved in, dominating the northern part of the country. The North was a Chinese province until 1,000 AD, when the Ly Dynasty became the first Vietnamese rulers. The Tran Dynasty followed them from 1225-1406. In 1426, Le Loi, with the help of tactician Nguyen Trai, removed the last Chinese. The Le Dynasty lasted until 1497.

In the South, the earliest evidence of civilization was Funan, a Hindu kingdom in the Mekong delta founded about the time of Jesus. Vietnam's southern tip was prime real estate for mercantile purposes, as it straddled the shipping lane between India and China.

From the dawn of history the South and North have been different. The South looked to the sea, the North to the land.

In the south, centered in Da Nang, the Champa Kingdom absorbed the old Hindu Funan culture, establishing its own identity. In 192 AD Cham rejected Chinese authority. The Champa were similar to the Maya, really no more than a loosely knit group of city states. Cham was never more than a moderate power, which continued to resist both the North Vietnamese dynasties and Imperial China. Much the same as Bali, which became a Hindu island in the midst of a Muslim sea, the kingdom absorbed the Hindu-Buddhist cosmology of India through Funan. Cham was never able to produce an agricultural surplus, and its kings paid tribute to the Chinese until the thirteenth century.

His nose seemingly stuck in the air, Marco Polo wrote in 1225 that the Champa *"paid tributes of elephants, and nothing but elephants."* Polo also noted that the King of Cham had 326 children, but his subjects were allowed no more than two wives.

In 1285, the Mongols invaded Vietnam and were thrown back by the Tran and the Champa fighting together. This resulted in more cooperation between the two, as well as intermarriage between the royal families. The Champa Kingdom officially lasted, in one form or another until 1725.

North of Cham, there were six different Vietnamese dynasties until 1802. The Nguyen family came to power and established the capital in Hue. Their rule coincided with the arrival of the French. Needless to say, it was doomed from the start.

The initial Euro settlement in Vietnam was Portuguese, just south of Da Nang. Antonio da Faria founded Faifo, now Hoi An, in 1535. The village was founded with the hope that it would become another Macao, but it never flourished. However, da Faria left a legacy in the name for the south of Vietnam that became *Cauchichina,* his interpretation of the Chinese: *Giao Chi.*

In August 1521, Cortez had conquered Montezuma at Tenochtitlan. Thus, Mexico and Central America became the colony, New Spain. By 1571, Miguel Lopez de Legazpi had overrun the Philippines. From here, the Spanish set sail west and found what they thought was virgin Indian territory: Champa.

Let us now travel in time to 1595.

Naos de China are beautiful, floating wooden fortresses. These Spanish galleons are crossing the Pacific to the *parian*, the market in Manila. They are bringing gold to trade in the Philippines. And they are bringing you, a Spanish sailor, as well as your compatriots, many of whom are anal-retentive products of the Inquisition. All return trade to Mexico is funneled through the "Acapulco Fair," a market set up for three months whenever a galleon returns.

Your name? Don Luis Perez das Marinas.

You? Having an ale at a sailor's bar just off the parian in old Manila. Squatting in the corner, the *sangleys* are haggling over how much they should pay you for gold. They have some new things, called "firecrackers," they want to trade. You are sweating, even in the shade. You haven't bathed since Champa. You don't know what toothpaste is, and you could care less if you did.

You have been back to Manila from Champa for three days, screwing Indians and drinking mostly. Now you've got a problem. You didn't sail back with anything except three urns of rice.

No Champa Indian gold.

And it is time to write up that trip report for your commander back in Acapulco.

You take another swig of ale, realizing there has been a strange tickling in your penis since noon. You mistakenly believe that you are the first Euro ship captain to set eyes on Vietnam.

You write... *"It is a land fertile in foodstuffs and cows and* oxen and very healthy in itself. It is not thickly populated and the people are swarthy, and heathens. In this kingdom there is no money or silver with which to sell anything; and in order to buy what they need, they exchange foodstuffs for cotton blankets and other things which they make for the purpose of buying and selling with each other.

"Nobody is allowed to go shod save only the king, and nobody can be married with more than two wives. They divide the year into six festivals. During the third festival, I saw them at the seaside, where they stay fishing for two months. They make merry catching enough fish to last them for a year, pickling it in their jars with just a little salt, and they eat it putrid in this manner. And they thrive very strong and lusty on this food.

"They say that the second festival also lasts two months. They spend the whole of this time singing to the exclusion of everything else, except when they are actually eating their meals. During this festival the women, of whatsoever condition they may be, have liberty to do what they like for the space of three days, during which they are not asked to account for their behavior.

"The fifth festival is when the king goes hunting elephants, of which there are many in this land. The last festival they celebrate is a tiger hunt. The tigers come to eat the buffaloes, which are tied to a tree in certain places. They place sentinels over them, so that when the tigers approach, the king is informed. And as soon as the king arrives the king gets ready with a great number of Indians and nets, and they do with tigers what they do with elephants. Surrounding them at once and killing them, there and then."

Time to insert the big lie, you think. Here in the middle.

Tell him what he wants to hear, back in Acapulco.

"It is the custom with these Indians that at the time when they are occupied with this hunt, the king and his wife send out a hundred or more Indians along the roads, with express order that *they should not return without filling two gold basins which they give them, full of human gall, which must be people from their own nation and not foreigners. And these emissaries do as they are told, not sparing anyone they meet, whether high or low degree. As soon as they can catch a person on the road, they tie him at once to a tree and cut out the gall. When all this is over the king and his wife wash with this human gall. And they say that in this way they cleanse themselves of their sins and their faults."*

You, as Don Luis Perez das Marinas, pause, looking up for penitence.

You sigh loudly.

"The justice of this people is peculiar, for they have no fixed criminal code, but only their personal opinions. And when the case is serious they investigate it with two witnesses. For very trifling and common offenses, they may cut off feet, hands, arms, or ears.

"They have another custom invented by the Devil himself, which is that when any leading personage dies, they cremate the body. They seize all the household servants, then they throw them alive into the flames so that they can serve them therewith in the other. Another custom which they have is that when the husband dies, they burn the wife with him. They say that this law was made to prevent wives from giving poisonous herbs to their husbands, for there are great witchcrafts and knaveries in these lands.

"They say that if the wife realizes that her husband will not live any longer than her, she will then take good care of his life, and his ease, and not dare to kill him with poison."

"INVISIBLE PLANT MANAGER"

For those wishing to expand their horizons concerning the shenanigans that occurred in Vietnam from 1880-1975, I recommend **Vietnam: A History** by Stanley Karnow, and **A Bright Shining Lie** by Neil Sheehan.

Since 1975 the country was more unified than at any time in its long history. By 1998, not many Americans would consider that Vietnam should be divided into two parts; anymore than they would think that about California.

Doi Moi, the new economic policy had significantly improved the economy in the early 1990s. However, the Vietnamese foreign investment boom began to wither because of bureaucracy and corruption by mid-decade, and further declined due to the Asian economic crisis in 1997.

Yet *Doi Moi* left a taste of freedom not known for decades.

In the autumn of 1997, the Communist Party Congress had to choose between the options of more reform in the economic arena or of tightening the state's power.

It chose the latter.

An article by R.J. Caldwell, "Vietnam Revisited" in the *San Diego Union-Tribune*, commented:

"American generals a generation ago professed to see light at the end of the Vietnam tunnel. They were, of course, wrong. Today, a latter generation of optimists is learning just how stubbornly disappointing Vietnam can be."

Although the forthcoming trip would be my first to Vietnam, I was already familiar with one communist nation in Asia. Between 1988 and 1992 I spent over four months in mainland China as the internal auditor for an electronics outfit which was one of the first American firms to manufacture its products in the People's Republic.

Over the years, my job eventually expanded into what in the 1950s they used to call a "Troubleshooter." The duties involved a wide scope, peering into the darkest nooks and crannies. By the end of the experience, I had seen enough mind-boggling things that I became regarded as an "Olde China Hand," at least within the company.

The China that I knew was hindered by the lack of a modern banking system. Businessmen paid cash; credit at non-usurious rates being a foreign concept. In 1992, corporate management came up with the radical *gwei-loh* idea, as in *gringo* idea, to pay our Chinese workers by check instead of "real money."

First, the employees complained to the communist "plant manager." A lot of good that did them, we never saw the official government plant manager although we mailed him $75 a month.

It was no bad deal for us. His $75 salary was, in effect, our only tax. No income tax, no sales tax, no value added tax. No customs duties, either. And the government built the plant for us; to suit. We rented it back from them, paid the workers a Christian Benevolence of 40 cents an hour but took back some for food and dormitory rent, and the workers each put in 50 hours a week with no provision for overtime pay.

Well, the big day arrived. We grandly parceled out our newly minted payroll checks.

The workers then stampeded out the factory gate for the local bank and deserted the premises, including the production floor. At the bank they formed a raucous line. But after the first 25 in line got their money, the bank shut its doors for the day.

Little did we realize that Chinese banks carried only $1,000 in cash. We resumed paying employees in the time-honored fashion. However, it wasn't simply our hardheaded *gwei-loh* quest for efficiency that precipitated this noble experiment. The payroll process went like this: We hand carried 400,000 Hong Kong dollars in a bag across into China because of the significant difference in the black market rate as opposed to the bank's for changing money into Chinese RNB. This necessitated meeting a Chinese black market broker and doing an uncomfortably large deal.

Eventually, for South China, the inevitable happened. A company employee got murdered on the plant premises. Whoever did it tried to burn the body to make it look like our employee died in a fire. The dead man was the one doing our business in the black market. The company's money was gone. We never found the murderer. That was when we came up with the great idea about the checks.

The situation seemed to be much the same for foreign businesses operating in Vietnam. Perhaps worse: The government wouldn't build your plant for you, and it would cost more than $75 a month in bribes to keep it running; not to mention taxes.

China's economy was far superior to Vietnam's. Still, in China, we paid three month's factory rent at the first of the quarter, about $6,000 in advance. This went out to our invisible plant manager, and it was a special deal just to keep him happy. He passed it along to the state, but before paying them he converted our rent money on the street. Of course the state had to recognize its own rate of exchange. Our invisible plant manager cleared about 15% on the deal. Also, while paying our rent one month at a time, he earned interest on the remainder.

A capitalistic wizard, eh?

The first time I entered the company plant in China, I

quickly found myself hopping over gaping holes in the floor. These were almost two feet in diameter. Down in the holes you could see colored wires running under the factory floor.

Curious, I asked, "What happened to the man-hole covers?"

The plant manager was Hong Kong Chinese. He said, "The workers steal them when we put them in."

I asked, "How much are they worth?"

As scrap steel, he figured, about two U.S. dollars each.

The covers that went on the floor were very heavy. You see, they were still sitting on all the floors in all the plants we had in Mexico, providing access and protection for the power lines. I had lifted up a few myself.

Walls, with security guards surrounded almost every foreign manufacturing plant in China. It was hard to imagine that anyone would risk so much trouble for such little reward. Was it that poverty in Asia was worse than in Mexico?

As for Vietnam, reports on the Internet indicated that even tourists could see the place changing before their eyes, perhaps coming to a crossroads. The question was: Would it become another Philippines? Or another Taiwan? Or a smaller version of China?

Despite the intelligence of her hard working people, today's Vietnam remained at the bottom of the Third World.

THE SOUTH

"GOOD MORNING, VIETNAM"

Somewhere above the South China Sea, I gazed out the window along the Cathay Pacific route from Hong Kong to Saigon.

As the sun broke the horizon on the other side of the aircraft with a powerful glare, the coast of Vietnam appeared.

A rock pile. Red-dirt trails crisscrossing, leaving crazy patterns. Not lush tropics, as I had expected. But I had heard that they had had a winter-long drought due to El Nino.

When we drove through the same area a week later, I would discover that this part of the coast was not typical. It looked much like Baja California; the mountains blocking out weather from the northeast in a pocket above Phan Thiet to Ca Na, where the coastline juts west.

That Vietnam, like Bali, was clothed uniformly in green was the first in a long line of misconceptions which would be shattered in the coming weeks.

The only other time I had laid eyes on Vietnam was also from an airplane, flying from Bangkok to Manila in 1981, only six years after reunification. I recall a huge bank of clouds resting just below the peaks on the Cambodian side. For a few minutes, we jetted over Vietnam's Central Highlands. Many clearings at that time were readily visible from above, each peppered with B-52 bomb craters.

Here in 1998 I was surprised to see no evidence of wartime destruction from the air. We shadowed Route One into Saigon. Now green rice paddies carpeted the landscape.

Shortly after 9 a.m., the plane set down at Tan Son Nhat airport. It taxied past row after row of half-circle, concrete shelters.

Built for American helicopters, almost all were empty.

Whereas in America we refer to "The Vietnam War," in Vietnam itself one had to differentiate. There have been many. America's involvement was known as "The War of Reunification." 1960-1975. As opposed to the "War Against Colonialism," 1935-1954, which was mainly against the French, but also the Japanese, as well as the Chinese Nationalists at the end of WW II. In addition, there were many famous wars and battles of the Vietnamese royalty against the ancient Chinese.

Recent conflicts were seldom mentioned in Vietnam.

The latest Chinese incursion in 1979 was 16 days of severe bloodletting along the northern border. Vietnam pushed China back.

Perhaps because beating up on foreign superpowers had become *de rigueur*, or perhaps because the current government was smart and wanted to get along with their socialist brothers, the clash with the People's Liberation Army of China was a non-event even at the Army Museum in Hanoi.

The Vietnamese equivalent of our "Vietnam" was not much alluded to either: The Cambodia adventure from 1978-1989. Pol Pot's Khmer Rouge Cambodian army had begun to cross the border even before the fall of Saigon in 1975 to raid hamlets in Vietnam, which were part of the ancient Cambodian Khmer Kingdom. Unlike the United States, Vietnam's foreign war ended in the achievement of most of its objectives: Getting rid of Pol Pot - a genocidal maniac on the order of Hitler and Stalin - and the institution of a friendly Cambodian regime next door.

But the Cambodian experience in no way corresponded to the Vietnamese government's anti-imperialist self-image.

Perhaps the war's most insidious effect was to divide North from South Vietnam even further at an early stage after re-unification. At that time, the North was devastated. In the capital, the powers that be decided to wage the Cambodian war mainly with Southern conscripts. The Khmer Rouge killed over 50,000 Vietnamese soldiers.

One person who managed to avoid conscript in Saigon in 1979 told me he watched his friends who did get drafted come home from Cambodia with a horde of worthless loot. That was what he remembered most about the time; other than his experience of avoiding military service. Moving, hiding. Bribing officials when caught.

Anyway, America's Vietnam War was just one of many for the Vietnamese.

It would be three weeks later, on the last night of our trip, when a young man would look at me at the Lac Viet Cafe in Hanoi, wondering at an injustice.

With a masculine sorrowful smile, he would say, "In the West, we are considered a country and a people who are good only at fighting."

By that time, I had just finished **The Sorrow of War**, by North Vietnamese author Bao Ninh. From this, as well as our travel experience, I understood what the young man was talking about. I knew it was a distorted image.

By then I had come to feel that the Vietnamese people were among the gentlest on Earth.

Once off the plane in Saigon the air was heavy, seeming to warm by the minute. Clearing immigration and customs took almost an hour, with unsmiling officials of the type you would expect in a socialist paradise. Under their dull, hardened stares, I forgot all about the mind-trip I had planned for myself.

That it could be 1966 all over again. Mud-caked combat boots. Ocher dirt. Scary land mines. Newsreel images from three decades past failed to materialize.

It was just another airport.

Petite said that it seemed relatively unchanged. She worked there in 1967 as a Pan Am counter agent. Most of it was at least recognizable to her.

But it wasn't just another airport to the thousands of Americans who landed there during the war. Or to the crowds who camped there in 1975 trying to escape before the Communists arrived.

Bao Ninh had been at Ton Son Nhat, too. It was eight years after Petite worked there that he fought in the final battle of a ten-year enlistment. The last battle of the War of Reunification.

Bao Ninh's entire scout platoon was wiped out at Ton San Nhat, except for him. His best friend, who had miraculously survived the entire conflict, was incinerated inside a tank during the airport assault on April 30, 1975. The last day.

Though the war was hopelessly lost, Southern ARVN commandos defending the airport counter-attacked in the afternoon. The ARVN troops were beaten back after furious fighting. The shooting slowed. Then it stopped.

Bao Ninh wrote his epic novel, **The Sorrow of War**, from the point of view of his protagonist; an NVA soldier named Kien.

"Kien lurched tiredly past a row of ARVN bodies, commandos in uniforms still wet from the rain, and stepped onto the polished granite stairs of the terminal."

Kien saw fellow NVA soldiers all about, mostly sleeping. He was past exhaustion, and he curled up on the floor. When he awoke, one of the others was looking disdainfully at him.

The soldier asked Kien, *"Shit, don't you know you've been sleeping next to a corpse? Couldn't you smell her?"*

Kien slowly turned his head to see where he'd been sleeping. A naked woman, her breasts firm and standing upright, her legs stretched out and open like scissors, her long hair covering her face, was near him, blocking the entry to the Customs office. She looked young. Her eyes were half-closed. No blood was visible.

"I was so tired I didn't notice her. I'll drag her away," said Kien.

"Leave her. Just don't touch her. Now the war's finished, it'll be bad luck to touch a corpse."

"I wonder why she's naked," said Kien.

"Beats me. We'd just shot those bastards over there and when we came in she was already lying there like that."

"Strange. The commandos are already stinking, yet she's still fresh..."

"Shut up! Gabbing on about stinking corpses while we're trying to eat."

Behind them they heard the Customs door swing open and a crashing noise. They turned to see a huge helmeted soldier tripping over the girl's body and dropping a crate of Saigon 33 Beer... The big man, embarrassed, got up and kicked at the body angrily, screaming at the dead girl. "You fucking prostitute, lying there showing it for everyone to see. Dare trip me over. Damn your ancestors! To hell with you!" he ranted.

Bao Ninh's novel was concerned with how war turned so many of his generation, who were far gentler than American kids of the same era, into something like the soldiers mentioned above.

I walked out into the heat, lifting a bulging suitcase, oblivious to any ghosts in attendance.

I heard, "Harry, Harry!" from among the throng outside.

It's Uncle! I recognized him from one of the family get-togethers to honor ancestors, which were held in L.A. He was now visiting his daughter in Saigon. Thin as a rail, he was still handsome, looking sporty in a bush hat at the age of seventy.

Uncle introduced us to his daughter, and to our driver-to-be whom he had contracted for a bargain $45 a day: Minh.

Minh was bowing and scraping.

We all took off in his van on a sunny morning, heading for the Rex Hotel at the center of downtown Saigon. Halfway there, we encountered tamarind trees and shaded boulevards. Out the window, I noticed a young lady with long shiny hair. She was bunched on the back of a motor scooter. Exotic, three-quarter-length purple gloves covered her arms. A medical mask covered half her face. Our bus pulled up to a traffic light and stopped. She and I were now at face level.

She turned and looked curiously.

I smiled.

She did not turn away. She seemed interested in not only me but the other members of our entourage. Away at the green light, I lost sight of her behind us in the traffic.

Petite explained, "They wear gloves to protect against the sun. Around here if you have brown skin it indicates that you're a field worker. Tanning is a Western thing."

The street passed by the side of an orange wall, aged with black. A sign said it was The Marie Curie something. I got the impression it was a shelter or an orphanage. Perhaps it was the old boarding school. It was the first French building I saw in Vietnam.

Vietnam's cities, I would find, were monuments to colonial architecture; Hanoi even more so than Saigon. In the rain, Hanoi's French Quarter looked like Paris.

Saigon looked Asian at all times due to the immense crunch of street traffic, like nothing in the U.S. Throngs of people, bicycles, motorbikes, more people, cars, busses, trucks. Dense, moving in a swollen stream. As a pedestrian, you stepped onto the street slowly to let the riders part around you. Then deliberately, all the way across, you would ford the river, one step at time; riders whizzing past you, inches away.

It was like a ballet, of sorts, to cross a street.

Minh stopped the van by the side of the Rex Hotel on a square which ran into a huge traffic circle. He got out and drew back the sliding door.

We hopped out.

A kid hustled over, holding out a hand. He used the other to grab onto a patch of hair on my arm.

I expected the waif to let go as I started walking toward the marble steps of the Rex.

"Hello where you from?" he said.

"Hello where you from?" he said.

He still had a handful of hair.

"Hello where you from?" he repeated.

I figured that batting him off would set a boorish precedent.

I said with bluster, "The United States."

My answer didn't register with the kid.

"Give me money," he whined.

He finally let go when he spotted the hotel bellman approaching, who would have swatted him away.

I would later learn that few of the street kids knew what the "United States" was. They knew it as "America."

"RIOTOUS, COLORFUL, DIZZY"

Petite got back to our cubicle at the Rex, as I awoke from a nap at 5 p.m. She had been around the corner, visiting relatives on Le Loi Street while I was bagged in our air-conditioned room.

Consulting the first item on my checklist, I was supposed to walk just outside the hotel and take in the Sunday night scene at the traffic rotary in front. The guidebook mentioned that on Sundays the intersection was a popular hangout for the young, parading around on their motorbikes. Back home, I had imagined plopping down at some sidewalk cafe, snapping a few shots of the action. I had brought along four rolls of 36 each, ASA 100 Kodak Gold, confident that 144 pictures would be ample.

Everyone told us before we left, "Take a lot of pictures."

I followed Petite into the elevator. We got off downstairs and walked into a room with exquisite bamboo paneling covering the walls and ceiling. To our left was a large round "calendar" that appeared to be the Oriental version of an Aztec sundial.

I limped down the hall, due to a tendon that hadn't healed since the previous summer when I hurt it playing outfield for an Over-40 baseball team at the age of 52. This slight limp produced a peculiar kind of walk: slow, easy, uneven. I am "Mutt" to Petite's short "Jeff." The contrast is noticeable, even in the States. For this reason we seemed to attract attention on the street. Even when there were other tourists around, we seemed to be wearing a target.

As we made our way to the lobby, I noticed that the hotel was entirely decorated in a mandarin motif. We passed a waiter dressed in Chinese lackey pajamas and a funky round hat, which was clearly a case of outdated hat technology. It wouldn't shield the sun, as my baseball cap would.

The first items I searched for before wandering outside were pictures of the "glory days." The Five O'Clock Follies. Journalists at the rooftop bar, gazing at the flash of nighttime combat on the horizon, figuring where they would go to cover the war the next day. A 33 Beer in one hand.

A color photograph in the lobby portrayed Party bosses who stayed at the Rex last year. Several other pictures of that occasion. Also, there was a photo of the French President and another of a woman, the French Minister of Culture.

On a far wall I noticed a pictorial history of the hotel.

"Ah, hah!" I thought.

In 1957 a multi-storied parking garage for the French ex-pat community occupied the site. There was a black-and-white photo of it. The next picture on the wall was titled simply: "Rex Hotel, 1961-1975." The hotel was built on the site of the garage and would become an American officer's billet, as well as the site of the press briefings by the military brass. Home to the infamous "body count."

The Rex was remodeled in the 1990s. There were numerous color photographs of the ribbon-cutting, etc. The remaining identifiable Yankee trait still around in 1998 was the hotel's use of American showerheads in its bathrooms. Every other Vietnamese hotel at which we stayed embraced inferior shower-room technology: A French, hand-held gizmo producing only a moderate dribble at optimum pressure.

I wrote in my diary, *"The hotel seems to have successfully erased the memory of its American experience. I'm not sure I blame them either."*

It occurred to me, as the doorman swung open the front door for us, that I had been in country for ten full hours (albeit asleep for half of it), and had not once thought about stepping on a leftover land mine. Preconceptions!

Outside at the bottom of the steps we landed on the corner of Nguyen Hue and Le Loi Streets. The two major boulevards were joined by a huge traffic circle. A public square, sort of a piazza-like park with a fountain, was to our left.

The light at six o'clock had just begun its evening pale, muted somewhat by the thick air. In the piazza a group of people hoisted a large board covered with brilliant red and yellow flowers. Motorbikes whizzed past, with young ladies bedecked in a riotous blend of silk pastel blouses. Oh, the different colors: Turquoise, chartreuse, lemon-orange, reddish-pink, sky blue.

And people, people, people. Everywhere.

Petite and I turned and looked at one another.

We shouted above the din in unison: "I'M DIZZY!"

I had thought it would be like this every night. It wasn't. That was the Sunday night crowd. More bedlam than usual.

I was now glad that I had gotten out of bed, instead of turning and falling asleep again when Petite had returned to the room. Per lifetime, the Creator issued only *one* first great impression of Vietnam. That was mine, and it was special.

Next, we waded into the traffic. The best policy for street crossing was to keep an eye out both ways and not to make sudden moves. Let them avoid you, something they did quite well.

We walked down the block to Petite's cousin's store. I became an instant millionaire by changing a hundred-dollar bill into 1,300,000 dong. From there, we retraced our steps to seek out Dong Khoi Street, the former Rue Catinat, the former Tu Do Street. We proceeded to the end of the block-long park toward what looked like an old French palace, now a municipal office for *Thanh Pho Ho Chi Minh*, the city's official name. We took a right. Ten minutes later we happened upon Notre Dame Cathedral, glowing majestically, with a crowd mingling in front of it.

Petite told me that we were walking toward where her mother used to live; in the wrong direction - away from the river.

We soon found Dong Khoi Street a few blocks in the other direction. The name meant "Uprising," as opposed to Tu Do, which meant "Freedom." We strolled past shops, art galleries, cafes, and modern hotels. I tried to figure out where the *Apocalypse Now* bar was. According to the guidebook, it was a popular ex-patriot watering hole.

Petite stopped several Vietnamese on the street to ask directions, none of whom had heard of such a strange sounding place, although according to the address I had it was in the neighborhood.

It was still warm in the evening, so we picked one of the few sidewalk establishments that we saw, *Cafe 13*, and sat down for a drink. The *333 Beer* was too sweet for my taste, but the people watching was superb. Cost: 10,000 dong, or $.77 a beer.

Back in the square across from the hotel, I was accosted by a ten-year-old boy. He grabbed onto my arm just as I tried to take a photo of the gigantic crown of glittering lights with "Rex" blazing across it. From the corner on the other side of the street, the sign artistically reflected off the waters of the fountain, where I had kneeled to get the best vantage for the picture.

The boy was demanding one U.S. dollar for a set of postcards.

Again I endured, and tugged him through the piazza, answering "No thank you" every two seconds. Finally it started getting painful.

I stopped and pinched the little bugger on the arm, *hard*.

I fully expected the child to start crying, or at least to scream out that the foreign gorilla had assaulted him. However, he didn't lighten his grip whatsoever. The physical contact seemed only to encourage him, until he spotted another tourist couple and he whisked away.

A tiny girl approached, lugging a bamboo-pole contraption with two balanced platforms hanging from each end, loaded with food. In this case, a coconut concoction.

She said something to Petite in Vietnamese.

My wife laughed heartily. "She claims *you* want me to buy one of her coconut things!"

It must have been mental telepathy. Petite obliged, agreeing to the 3,000 price, after which the girl persuaded my wife to let her keep the change from a 5,000.

We were knowing suckers the whole time in Vietnam, interested in encouraging people on the street who worked for their money instead of begging.

Once back in the hotel room, we both had difficulty sleeping. I assumed it was due to the stimulus and elation of finally being there.

"TIME WARP"

Monday, our first full day, was museum day.

I had compiled a lengthy list: The art museum, the war crimes museum, the history museum of course, with its botanical gardens. The revolutionary museum. Also on the list, a couple of not-exactly-museums: Cercle Sportif and the former Presidential Palace, now known as Reunification Palace.

Naturally it turned out that on Mondays all the museums were closed.

We weren't planning on seeing them all in one day, anyway. The list was for the whole week, apart from the day trip I had planned for the Cu Chi tunnels, which were a couple of hours out of Saigon.

I was not the least bit interested in the Presidential Palace. We had driven by it on the way in from the airport. Sixties Kitsch. However, it was one of the few places open on Mondays.

Saigon was one of those "great cities to walk around in."

We were ten minutes from the Rex, halfway to the Palace, when we happened upon a faded white villa with two rusted jets parked on the front lawn. We decided to check it out.

It was the Revolutionary Museum. There was a conference going on in the main building. However, a separate wing devoted to the 1968 Tet offensive was open.

A college-aged girl sat by the entrance. No fee.

As with most of the war photos I saw in Vietnamese museums these were very grainy; black and white, of worse quality than the ones Matthew Brady took with a flash pan during *our* civil war. Must have been the Russki film. Blurry images of ghost-like army units. Civilian sympathizers in *Sai Gon*.

The captions were only in Vietnamese. Petite translated.

"Heroes of the revolution. A man lifting a trap door to show where he hid some rockets out of sight of wayward American imperialists or Saigon puppet troops."

A group of letters caught my eye. They were from U.S. Army soldiers, captured during Tet '68 while on a convoy just outside of Cu Chi. One was a Black American, his letter separated from the others with additional verbiage about the Black Experience. Aside from that, all four letters contained the exact wording; apologizing for fighting the Vietnamese people. The American soldiers admitting the errors of their sinful ways.

Also, there was a VC phys-war pamphlet dropped on American soldiers that read:

GET OUT OF THE SUN. **GO HOME!**

Good propaganda. Simple. Neat.

The one-sidedness was humorous.

Petite thought so, too. She had always told me that the Communists had the best propaganda, something at which they excelled. But she had been referring to propaganda for folks in the rice paddies. It appeared to me that they had good propaganda to hand out for just about anyone, from U.S. soldiers to utopian-minded university professors.

Our next stop was the palace. But we had lingered too long. It was closed for lunch at 11:00 a.m. So we strolled by the park that it was in. Petite went inside an art gallery, trying to find the phone number of one of her friends. After that, we took a left at the end of the park, onto Nguyen Thi Minh Khai Street. Petite pointed out a famous Catholic girl's school across the street. It was letting out for lunch with a swarm of young ladies on bicycles, all wearing white *ao dais*, the Vietnamese national dress that was similar to a pants suit and seemed to make anyone look good.

Down the block was the old Cercle Sportif, a sports club that remained a symbol of colonial exclusion policies. It had another name now. Didn't catch it.

The old clubhouse fronted the street. It was open only at night, used primarily as an auditorium. At the rear of this building, in a shaded open space we watched a competitive girl's volleyball game. Pepsi umbrellas lined the courtside. A logo on the banner indicated that this was part of a tournament for the city championship. To our left were tennis courts, which appeared newly refurbished. Heineken signs adorned the backcourt fences.

Across the way was an Olympic swimming pool set beneath a hill in a pleasant setting above the rest of the complex.

On the way out, we passed two boys throwing horseshoes. The tennis courts were almost full. Petite translated a price list posted by the horseshoe pit. It cost 500 dong a day ($.03) to use the swimming pool.

I had worked up a pouring sweat, out and about for three hours. I wanted a drink. Petite was hungry. We found a food place; a typical Asian alleyway shack with a parachute awning over the tables and a corrugated metal roof covering the kitchen.

I had a Tiger beer, the brand Uncle drank, and it tasted better than 333. Even sitting in this converted alley, I took a few pictures. There were photo opportunities in Vietnam, it seemed, every thirty seconds.

A bicycle. Bamboo. A cone-hat on the handlebars. Tropical flowers and a pink and blue parachute filtering the sun. In the background a French colonial home, now abandoned and seedy. Petite's pale cotton vest with patterns of pearls.

"Did the flash go off?" I asked her, after I kneeling to get the proper angle and snapping it.

"Didn't see it," she said.

That one could have been a contender. Oh, well.

Heading down the street alone toward the Presidential Palace, I glanced back, slightly worried. Petite was still arguing with a cyclo driver over the fee to take her back to the Rex. Two other drivers had gathered to watch, surrounding her.

I turned and headed back. I had this "thing" about getting surrounded in the Orient.

But Petite saw me coming. She laughed from across the street, waving me away.

No worries, I supposed.

Later Petite explained to me that people on the street were not trying to hurt you. You were simply entertainment fodder, according to her. They couldn't afford the movies.

At the Reunification Palace, I was directed to a waiting area by the front steps. Soon another American joined me. Surprise. He was from Virginia, on vacation. Too young to have remembered the war; 31 years old.

A Vietnamese woman guide led us to the first room on our quasi-private English-speaking tour. She was friendly.

The room looked like a banquet hall in Las Vegas. Chandeliers, the whole bit.

"Pictures?" she asked.

Not for me, but the Virginian headed toward the far end. The guide and I were now alone.

Speaking slowly and distinctly, I said to her in a whispery, conspiratorial voice, "You mentioned that Diem was the 'President of the puppet Saigon regime'... My wife is from the South, and she told me that people here, even during the war, respected Ho Chi Minh as a genuine patriot. But they also felt the same way about Diem. I think that the Southerners considered both of them nationalists."

The guide flinched. "It's just a job," her look seemed to say. She was glad to spot a fiftyish Aussie couple and three *Viet Kieu* from California, ex-patriot Vietnamese, walking up to join our tour, as the Virginian reappeared.

One of the *Viet Kieu* led the way downstairs, lugging a camcorder.

Overkill, it appeared to me.

The basement of the Palace was a warren of passageways, some blocked off, with bunkers and rooms with a lot of maps. The maps showed NVA, VC, ARVN, and U.S. positions. I didn't figure the Communist strongholds would have been marked as "Liberated Areas" back in the glory days. They were now. I was busy trying to locate Khe Sanh, so I could see how the NVA surrounded it. The Aussie woman on the tour came and got me. Everyone else had moved on.

"Train's pulled outter the station, mate."

We hooked a lucky left on the first intersecting passageway and caught up with the group, who were in front of a dark office-sized room staring at electrical equipment.

I leaned over for a peek.

Deja Vu!

A "low-level" scanner. Ohmmeters out the butt, a little speaker setup. Exactly like some of our equipment at ASA Field Station Berlin in the late 1960s, all sitting on a vintage peeled gray Army-issue desk of the same era.

Again, I had to catch up. The Aussie hadn't bothered this time. I found them in the next room up. It was photo opportunity time. A black leather chair. Glass top desk. Big map at the rear and a sign on the desk top.

Phong Chi Huy
Commanding Room

The Virginian and I traded cameras for this. It seemed to me that I was delivering a stern glare from behind the desk, pointing a forefinger authoritatively at the camera, my other hand gripping the phone as if commanding the field officers to change the order of battle.

The photo actually turned out with a literal tongue in cheek, in place of the "killer" stare I was trying so hard to project at the time.

Before we left I noted that the general tenor of the room seemed to almost scream for a flag or two, but there were none.

Our group took the outdoor staircase up several floors, a hot-humid climb in the afternoon. There were libraries with both English and Vietnamese books. More banquet halls. A mezzanine on each floor. Medieval weapons on display. And a large communications center with a "direct line to Washington," as the guide put it. A beautiful red lacquer painting covered one wall in an ornate room where diplomats presented their credentials to the South Vietnamese government.

Last but not least we came upon a 1960s Swinging cocktail lounge in bold Playboy Bunny pink and white, with cherry-red barstools and heavy inlaid speakers. Only the cages for the go-go girls were absent.

Rock the Casbah, baby.

Ho Chi Minh likely did not have one of those.

After a last set of stairs, we were on the rooftop.

I admired the view of a battle tank sitting on a side lawn and the sight of the huge double boulevard running through the park across the street and up to the front gate of the Palace.

On the other side, at some time during a second cigarette, I glanced down to see two huge circles painted on a roof below. These marked the spots where the NVA sent a couple of rounds through the ceiling. We had already visited the room where General "Big" Minh, president for two days, performed his final presidential duty.

"I have been waiting since early this morning to transfer power to you," Big Minh told Bui Tin, the NVA general, on April 30, 1975.

General Bui answered, *"Your power has crumbled. You cannot give up what you do not have."*

This magnanimous reply foreshadowed what was to come.

I stood on the breezy rooftop and realized that I had just visited a time warp in the person of this building. The curators had done a great job in maintaining the look and feel of an era I knew so well.

The guide summoned our group.

She led the way into a screening room.

I secured a seat with room on either side. At least, the movie room was air-conditioned.

We watched a black and white film made in France in the 1970s. French could be heard faintly beneath an English overdub. First, a gloating description of the fall of Saigon in 1975. Then a tank, perhaps the one on display outside, breaking down the fence outside the Palace. NVA soldiers riding trucks through the streets, many onlookers waving.

The film got even scratchier when it showed a French colonial official handing over power to a haughty Japanese general in 1940. On to a Japanese handing his sword to a haughty Chinese general after World War II. Chinese soldiers goose-stepping in Hanoi. The French once more. Dien Bien Phu in 1954. "Uncle Ho," *Bac Ho*, taking over in the North, with the country divided at the Seventeenth Parallel. President Diem in the South. The Americans coming into the conflict.

At this point, the film had shown four sets of foreign soldiers in Vietnam within a quarter century.

A color film clip now appeared on the screen. Taken from

the rear of an American bomber, it pictured a low straight-line bombing run; a trail of explosions one after another on a jungle mountainside, which passed over and wasted a couple of thatched huts, then continued above the virgin canopy for awhile. Bombing away. A seemingly useless effort to put a line of holes in the jungle.

There was no narration during this scene. None was needed. It was stupidity without logic.

The Virginian got up and left quietly. Then the *Viet Kieu* took off, but I decided to stick it out.

Nothing of note was shown in the last five minutes. Only three of us remained at the end, when the guide came in and announced that the tour was officially over.

We thanked her. I slipped her 10,000.

I followed the Australian couple out.

Along the way down the four-floor descent in the stairwell, the Aussie wife kept repeating to her husband, *"Bloody disgusting what the Americans did here!"*

After which, she never failed to glance back at me with her steely eyes.

I was not sure what reaction she expected. I didn't bother telling her I agreed, assuming she was referring to the bombing scene, which I supposed she was. Nothing else had been particularly inflammatory regarding the Americans.

But on the fifteen-minute walk to the Rex Hotel, it started to bother me how this film could produce such intemperate reactions from a citizen of a country that fought the war on the same side that we did. This, despite the fact that I had to admit that the documentary had shown nothing that was untrue as far as I could tell.

Still, the accusatory response from the Aussie was surprising.

"GOOD PROPAGANDA"

The next day, Tuesday, we got off to an early start. Minh drove Petite, Uncle in his debonair safari hat, and me out of Saigon to the Cu Chi tunnels.

I was busy in the back of the van, taking in the scenery as we proceeded through grimy Saigon suburbs and into a world of brilliant green paddies and water buffalo. Uncle's daughter had warned us that he was planning to ask if he could accompany us on our trip from Saigon to Hue. Petite thought, perhaps hopefully, that I would nix the idea immediately.

But I said, "Let's play it by ear."

So we did exactly that. Uncle talked for two hours straight, non-stop, hardly coming up for air until we rolled into Ben Duoc. Minh was playing Vietnamese popular-rock songs on the tape deck. So the music, as well as the substantial number of road decibels, covered up most of the rabid conversation up front.

There were two Cu Chi tunnel sites. Ben Dinh was the one closer to Saigon, the one included on most of the tours. We had air-conditioned wheels. Who needed tourist busses? Not us. Ben Duoc, a second site 15 kilometers beyond, had the *"dubious additional attractions of a grounded helicopter and a firing range,"* according to the guidebook.

Hot dogeys.

Petite paid for two tickets at the entrance to Ben Duoc.

Hearing rifle fire, I glanced longingly toward the range.

"Whew!" Petite said, referring to Uncle's performance.

Uncle and Minh settled in at an outdoor table at the restaurant. Both refused to take the tour. Uncle had plopped down his cooler filled with ice-cold beer and bottled water. The way to go in Vietnam was to act like you were the Emperor just in from Paris; or convince the employees that, at the very least, you owned the place. Then you could get away with whatever you wanted to within legal bounds.

I looked back at them. Uncle was talking to Minh.

We followed the guide into a forest of tall trees, all with narrow trunks. He said something in Vietnamese. Petite translated.

"Bomb craters."

It was not thick jungle, more like thick forest. A canopy of cedars filtered the sun. The dirt was sufficiently red even for my tastes. Beautiful, but with a certain claustrophobia about it if you imagined yourself pacing among these hardwoods on search and destroy, as I imagined myself. I glanced at a B-52 hole the guide was talking about. It was now a vine-covered crater.

Our guide quickly vanished up the trail, trotting ahead to wherever.

I said, "Did we sign up for a race?"

Petite said, "Wait a minute. Do you want an English-speaking guide? I know they have one."

"Sure."

We had to pay an additional amount and I forked over the cash.

Out walked Guide Number Two, who didn't look all that pleased about it as he trotted past, telling us to hurry along. But I was grateful to have him lead the way in case there was unexploded ordnance still about.

When Petite and I moseyed up, he was standing beside a stiff-looking exhibit of wooden guerrilla figures.

VC disguised as totem poles, perhaps?

"You take pictures!" the guide barked.

"Uh, no thanks."

He did not seem pleased with my answer. I felt it getting hostile, but now he joined us on our stroll to the next stop and hadn't sprinted ahead. He looked more Chinese than Vietnamese; thick eyebrows resembling Chou En Lai, Mao's right-hand man.

"Go ahead. Walk in front, if you want to," I told him. "Be our Minesweeper!"

He thought this was hilarious and actually laughed.

Then I asked him where he was from.

He got serious again and told me he was from a village twenty klicks away. Yes, he was VC. He had fought here during the war.

Copacetic, I thought.

We arrived at a thatched hut, open on three sides. An auditorium. It seated about thirty but it was deserted. Petite and I plopped into front row chairs.

The television was a small screen Sony. I think it was a Korean tape deck. We slid our chairs up a bit, while the guide fiddled with a tape. I noticed a colorful mural to one side depicting crazed GIs, as well as a helicopter raining bullets. But no forest.

As in most areas of heavy fighting, this one looked completely different than it did during the 1970s. The Americans had flattened the landscape. The guide pointed out that there were still original trees a few kilometers away on the former Michelin rubber plantation.

On the other side of the television was a large layout of the area. The entire Cu Chi system. The guide pointed out his village without hesitation, after I asked him to.

The Viet Minh first dug the legendary tunnels in the late 1940s. By 1965, the Viet Cong in this predominately anti-government area had extended them to total 160 miles of tunnels snaking below the red clay. Some emerged on the banks of the

Saigon River a few miles away. The Americans knew the opposite side of the river as the "Iron Triangle." The VC had dug below the U.S. Army base at Cu Chi, as well.

The area was a primary focus of attention mostly from 1966 to 1968. In January 1967, Operation Cedar Falls did just what the name implied. Defoliants and bulldozers were used to raze the countryside. The local population was forced into resettlement camps, which were euphemistically referred to as "strategic hamlets." Later, B-52 carpet-bombing leveled the district, but the communist troops remained in their tunnels and became instrumental in the attack on Saigon during the Tet Offensive.

This offensive decimated the Viet Cong, and the NVA replaced it. About 12,000 people died in this part of the countryside during the American War.

Our guide was not one of them. He cursed and ripped out the first tape he had stuffed into the machine. His audience was attentive, eager, on the edge of our seats, literally, but he had put in the French-language version.

During the screening of this masterpiece, a grainy 1967 propaganda film, Petite and I were by ourselves. One of her brothers-in-law had been an ARVN colonel who spent five years in "re-education" camps north and west of Hanoi. I had talked to him about it several times. Petite was his sponsor to the United States. He lived with us for awhile when he first arrived in San Diego in 1981. Sitting in Cu Chi watching a blatant propaganda film, it was easy to imagine that we were being "re-educated."

A classic line from the film:

"On and on, the American shells pounded Mother Earth!"

The television screen showed flying palm trees.

I glanced back. The guide, swinging on a hammock in the shade with his eyes closed, was probably dreaming of the glory days; just exactly how he might have gone about cutting the fat American's throat. The one who was sitting where I was.

Mercifully, the film ended. Its effect on me was to kill the desire to see any more official history exhibits. Viewing this thing, you might have figured that the VC had never mortared Mother Earth.

At this point another couple joined our tour. An Aussie and his wife, originally from the Philippines. The guide told them that they would see the film after completing the rest of the tour.

The five of us set off on a dirt trail through the woods. The guide stopped a short while later. He went just off the trail and cleared away some shrubs and leaves. Now smiling for a change, dusting away, he revealed a trap door perfectly camouflaged. He raised it to show a small black hole. An actual entrance; not one enlarged for the tourist trade.

It looked like a tight fit even for Petite at 4 feet, 10 inches, and 90 pounds.

He explained that he and his compatriots used to attach bars of GI soap beneath such hatches and that this would cover the scent from the dogs that GIs used to sniff out tunnels.

Everyone in the group got a chuckle out of that.

There were three levels of tunnels. The bomb craters, which seemed to be everywhere, were evidence of the B-52 attacks. The guide said that the shells would cave in the top two levels.

Bottlenecks were built into the system. The guide said, "We put places in each tunnel even more narrow than the openings in order to keep out the fat American soldiers."

I asked him about the "tunnel rats," small-stature GIs whose job was to climb down into them.

The guide said, "They never get far."

I believed it. "Far" being a relative, my guess was that the Americans never grasped the true extent of these tunnels, a reality that may have been almost incomprehensible from the Western point of view at the time.

They knew there was a tunnel system. But this?

Hospitals, mess halls, kitchens, command bunkers, dormitories, latrines, water wells. One hundred sixty miles worth on three different levels?

From **The Rough Guide**:

"The tunnels were foul smelling, and became so hot in the early afternoon that inhabitants had to lie on the floor in order to get enough oxygen to breathe. The darkness was so profound that some long-term dwellers suffered temporary blindness upon reaching the surface. At times it was necessary to stay below ground for weeks on end, in living quarters shared with bats, rats, snakes, scorpions, centipedes, and fire ants. Some of these unwelcome guests were co-opted to the cause: boxes full of scorpions and hollow bamboo sticks containing vipers were secreted where GIs might unwittingly knock them over.

Maverick war correspondent Wilfred Burchett, traveling with the NLF in 1964, found his Western girth a distinct impediment: 'On one occasion I got stuck passing from one tunnel section to another. In what seemed a dead end, a rectangular plug was pulled out from the other side. With some of them pulling my head, some my arms and some pushing my buttocks from behind, I managed to get through... I was then transferred to another tunnel entrance built especially to accommodate a bulky unit cook.'

*Maintaining morale was a constant challenge, one met in part by performing troupes that toured the tunnels; though their politically-correct songs – '**He who comes to Cu Chi, the Bronze Fortress in the Land of Iron, will count the crimes accumulated by the Enemy**' was one - were hardly in Bob Hope's league."*

The tunnels were full of false walls and airtight chambers to protect the soldiers from tear gas, water, shrapnel, and so forth.

In addition to snakes and poisoned pungi sticks, homemade bombs made from discarded soda cans waited to blow off a tunnel rat's...

Well, perhaps the slogan of the tunnel rats themselves said it all: **Insigni Non Gratum Anus Rodentum.**

"Not worth a rat's ass."

We walked farther into the woods and came to the first tunnel we would enter. It was Vietnam's answer to Disneyland. A gaping hole that would fit the fattest tourist who ever walked the planet, steps that led down, a gothic archway supported by concrete walls. Bare light bulbs to brighten the way.

It was fun creeping along inside, bent over like Old Man Time. We came to an underground aid station, took some pictures, and soon were above ground again.

The guide led us to another large opening and we scrambled through it like veterans until we got to a command bunker. A table was set up with three "Viet Cong," their wooden eyes perpetually fixed on the commander figure at the head of the table. In dim light, the figurines were more life-like than ones we had seen at the beginning of the tour. The guide handed Petite a green camouflage cap to wear. She "stood tall" beside Fearless Leader at the head of the table while I preserved the scene for posterity.

In a corner of the room was a menacing display of pungi sticks set inside a cement rectangle. Personally grateful that we would now not leave the country without seeing at least one set of these, I dutifully snapped another photograph.

Petite translated the writing on a red and gold banner on the wall: *"Nothing Is More Precious Than Independence & Freedom."*

Who could argue with that?

We were out of the hole again, traipsing about for several minutes. The tour had lasted over an hour, it was getting toward noon, and even on the shady trail there was only one word for it.

Hot.

The guide halted the troops in front of yet another opening.

He said, "The tour is over now, unless you wish to sample some of the food that we ate during that time." He pointed toward the stairs leading down.

The Aussie seemed noncommittal and his Filipina wife pawed the ground with her tennis shoe. Petite looked hot and tired. I was dripping sweat, as usual, and was never an "adventurous eater."

But for unknown reasons, I said, "Why *not*?"

The five of us trudged into an underground mess hall.

The guide poured us each a cup of tea, and handed out portions of ground tapioca. When mixed with a little sugar, it almost tasted good.

The guide did not partake except for tea. As the rest of us were chewing away vigorously, he said, "Tapioca gives us *energy*." Then assuming the classic rifleman's stance, eyes glazing over, he added, "To kill the enemy!"

He started firing off imaginary rounds.

When he snapped out of it, it was eerie. I felt that in ten seconds his mind had taken him back. That it was no act. That the prideful look on his face reflected the struggle, the hardship, the bravery, and the comradeship he had experienced.

The chatter among the five of us sitting around the underground table became especially light and friendly.

Then the Filipina, perhaps in an attempt to impress the guide, told us how her country had suffered under the U.S. just as the Vietnamese had. How brave Filipinos had fought for freedom using pitchforks and such, and had stood up to Yankee firepower - rifles and artillery - during the insurrection.

"We were only defeated by their modern guns," she explained, brushing at a tear that was about to form.

I said, "Well, perhaps! But I can't *take* much more

hypocrisy! Say *you* had the weapons and we didn't, wouldn't you have used them on *us*?" I asked.

There was a bit of nervous laughter from her husband, who seemed embarrassed. His wife threw back her head without saying anything. For whatever reason, the guide now seemed to take my side of the issue.

We sat around for another five minutes. Conversation quickly returned to normal, the tension dissipated. When we got above ground I thanked the guide, tipped him, and told him truthfully that we were lucky to have had him show us around.

He said that he was happy that there was peace, and he was glad that foreigners came to Cu Chi, and many nice people were among the tourists. He seemed to be including us in that group.

We waved good-bye as he led the Aussies back through the forest to the picture show.

What bothered me was that here was a second instance in two short days where I encountered an emotional anti-American outburst from a citizen of a supposedly "friendly" country. It was the type of thing I might have expected from a Vietnamese who had lost part of his family to the American war, or perhaps from a young student in Vietnam who didn't know any better.

What good propaganda they have, I thought, to produce such reaction from people who have the freedom to see both sides of the story. That night I wrote in my diary:

"I came to realize how really easy it is to rewrite history."

Not an original thought. Yet, a watermark for me. One cliche that finally hit home. History has always been rewritten. History has always been subjective, distorted.

Amnesia was an integral part of every nation's building process.

Later in the trip we would visit My Lai, the site of an

American atrocity. On March 16, 1968, American soldiers entered a village on a sweep and destroy mission. Before the day was out they raped women, mutilated bodies, executed 500 non-combatants including babies, and left many dead and dying piled in an irrigation ditch.

In order to get a better understanding of how this happened, I later read **Four Hours In My Lai**, the authoritative account of the massacre written by Michael Bilton and Kevin Sim.

The horror of war was something that, as I have mentioned, I chose not to experience. I believed no one could ever know how he would react in that situation without such experience.

One thing I learned from the book was that My Lai was not an isolated aberration that stood alone in American history. It was rare, but it had happened before. Part of our own selective historic erasure.

For the record:

"We must act with vindictive earnestness against the Sioux, even to the extermination of men, women and children. Nothing else will reach the root of the case."
Gen. William Sherman to Gen. U.S. Grant

"The American soldier, in officially sanctioned wrath, is a thing so ugly and dangerous that it would take a Kipling to describe him."
Lt. James Blount, on the behavior in the Philippines in 1900

"I want no prisoners. I wish you to kill and burn - the more you kill and burn the better it will please me."
Gen. Jake Smith's orders in 1901 before the attack on Samar
(During the Philippine War, 1898-1902, 10,000 to 20,000 insurgents and some 200,000 civilians died).

"We shot prisoners in cold blood, wiped out hospitals, strafed lifeboats, killed or mistreated enemy civilians, finished off the enemy wounded, tossed the dying into a hole with the dead, and in the Pacific boiled flesh off enemy skulls to make table ornaments for sweethearts, or carved their bones into letter openers."
E.L. Jones on World War II

"It was this Nazi kind of thing. We didn't go there to be Nazis. At least none of the people I knew went there to be Nazis. I didn't go there to be a Nazi."
A GI at My Lai

The two things I most enjoyed about this journey were the Vietnamese people themselves and the country's scenery.

What I disliked most was the hypocrisy of its government. The passages above were inserted to show that selective amnesia was neither a particularly Vietnamese trait, nor was it out of the ordinary.

Back home in San Diego, I asked a young man who lived down the street if he remembered the name "My Lai" from his high school history classes.

"I think so," he said. "Didn't that have something to do with Lt. Kelly, or something?"

Yes, good propaganda was everywhere.

46

"CLUELESS"

Petite and I headed back toward the entrance at Cu Chi.

Soon the trail split in two, and I made a wrong choice. Firing started up at the rifle range. We doubled back and walked toward the distant sound of gunfire.

I stumbled along, wondering about the Filipina.

After all we did for the Philippines, I thought.

Uncle was into a third Tiger beer when we got back to the restaurant. I noted that Minh the driver had been drinking only bottled water. We still had a long way to go in the afternoon because we planned to drop by a relative's house and visit Petite's parents' graves for a short ceremony. Then back into Saigon at rush hour.

First.

Uncle popped a cold Tiger for me. A waitress stopped by to see if we wanted to buy something. I got Petite a Pepsi.

In English, I told Uncle and Minh that back in the army I qualified on the range as an 'Expert' marksman.

I told them I'd been looking forward to this and mentioned my grandma, a regarded West Texas markswoman after the turn of the century. I said it was my treat if they wanted to join me on the range.

Uncle understood at least the last part, he shook his head vigorously.

Minh had a silly grin that was hard to decipher.

I asked Petite, "Please translate the invitation to Minh."

His hands started going crazy.

Petite said, "Guns frighten him."

We left Minh to guard our stuff at the restaurant. Uncle and Petite walked with me to watch the exhibition and take pictures. We went into a shack. I signed the waiver, and found out it cost one Yankee dollar per bullet.

I had envisioned firing a full clip on automatic until then.

The fellow at the desk took my five dollars. Reaching for an M-16, he said, "American?"

Forget about it. "Give me an AK," I told him.

I had never shot an AK-47 before.

He loaded a clip with five rounds, and grabbed a rifle. Petite and I followed him out the door. Uncle elected to view at a safe distance on the other side of the fence.

I was a little nervous after the all the bragging and name-dropping even if they hadn't understood a word.

Soon peering through the eyepiece, I lined the sight on a target 100 yards away. Mr. Tiger painted on it. I raised an elbow. The sight found the head above mid-target. Steady...

Bang.

Nailed it.

I looked to Petite for confirmation.

Face down, she fiddled with our camera.

So I smiled at the fellow who worked at the range, who wore a disgusted look on his face, shaking his head.

Apparently the Communist was trying to rule my good shot away, like they did in the Olympics. I turned to the business at hand.

Bang. Bang. Bang.

I was madly pulling the trigger but the thing had jammed.

The guy came over. He jerked out the clip, adjusted the last bullet, reloaded the clip, and put the AK-47 back in the rifle rest.

"Four shots low," he said disapprovingly.

I said, "Bullshit."

He was correct on the last three. Even with the rifle rest I had been unsteady on rapid fire. Was it the beer? The heat? I knew I'd hit the first shot, though.

"All low!" he repeated.

Okay! I'll adjust.

I checked for breeze but the air was still.

The sight was at the top edge of the target and I raised it just a tad in case I had been firing low... Arms correct. Smoothly...

Bang.

Dirt kicked up above the target.

"High!" the Communist said.

No Shit, Sherlock.

Petite was no help. She couldn't tell whether I'd hit anything, and didn't care anyway. We made our way back to the shack, where the rifle range guy insisted that I try a full clip on automatic. Something like 17 rounds. Implying that I might be able to hit something if I did that.

Suckers play, no doubt.

I said, "The fish aren't biting on that one today."

I tried to confirm my lone hit with Uncle when we got to the van, but he had been so far away that he could hardly make out the target.

Petite started telling us how she had learned to shoot a rifle when she was in high school. Madame Nhu had made her learn that precious skill in some patriotic self-defense program set up in the 1960s. I tried to imagine Petite lugging a heavy weapon. The mental image did not compute.

This Is My Rifle
This Is My Gun
This One's For Fighting
This One's For Fun
Ft. Leonard Wood, Feb. 1966

"Private Truman, what is the Spirit of the Bayonet?"
"To Keee-al, Ser-geant!"
Ft. Leonard Wood, Mar. 1966

The energy level was starting to fade. I hadn't slept more than five hours a night since we'd been in Saigon. I was an eight-hour guy. So on the way to the relatives house, I was thinking about weird past experiences, such as the above. Back in another lifetime in basic training with a Texas accent, I was pretty good at "To Keee-al, Ser-geant," knowing I'd soon be killing cases of Beck's Bier rather than people, and wouldn't need a bayonet for that.

Sitting in the back of the bus an hour out of Cu Chi, I realized that perhaps I had moved to California because of basic training. It was zero degrees in Missouri at Fort Leonard Wood in February 1966. A typical basic training compound, one of the most depressing places I've ever been to. My favorite song on the jukebox in the canteen was "California Dreaming."

"All the leaves are brown and the sky is gray."

In 1966 there was the sad sack private, slumped in the corner feeling sorry for himself with four years to go, wondering if it would ever end. And if it did, he was headed out West.

I snapped out of this reverie when Minh the driver turned off the paved road and onto a dirt track running alongside a canal.

We were in Hoc Mon, a government development to house people outside the city. There was no rent. The houses were typical of others in the South, where it never got cold. Northern housing was more substantial.

We pulled up to Petite's mother's brother's wife's house. A swarm of fourteen friendly folks of all ages came out to greet us.

Going in, I bumped my head on a piece of corrugated metal roofing. The children thought I had done it for their entertainment. Someone handed me a cold beer.

The house was small. It had whitewashed wood walls and a nice pinkish-orange tile floor. I took a seat on the sofa, where the men had gathered to drink and chain smoke.

One of them named Kiet spoke English. He had been assigned to entertain me. He was thin, dressed in a white short-sleeved shirt with black pants. Soft spoken. He seemed to have a matter-of-fact personality.

The first thing Kiet said was, "I worked with the 101st Airborne as a translator."

It meant he was anti-Communist.

Quite a few people, including some in the North, would let you know where they stood when you first met.

Kiet said he spent a short time in a reeducation camp after the war. But the worst part was that for a long time the government had discriminated against Southern war veterans when handing out jobs. Only recently, he had landed a job in Saigon; riding his bicycle an hour and a half each way to work.

It made me feel bad. He was about the same age I was. And I used to bitch about half-hour commutes in my air-conditioned car.

Since 1975, Kiet had tried to move his family to the States, with no success. He said the government had bulldozed ARVN military cemeteries around Saigon.

Kiet's son sat with us. In his twenties, he told me he worked for Coca-Cola. I asked him how long the company had been in Vietnam.

The son said, "Five years."

The same as all the American companies which moved back into Vietnam.

I asked Kiet how much he got paid.

"$100 a month," he answered.

Exactly the salary the workers at the Rex earned.

Kiet was bitter about the lack of opportunity.

I asked, "Surely things have gotten better in the past five years, haven't they?"

He admitted that it was better now.

Then he got up in order to peddle to work. He said the worst thing was coming back home in the darkness.

Once he was gone, there was no one who spoke English.

Petite was busy handing out money. Uncle had pulled her over for what I assumed was grandfatherly advice on gifting etiquette. It was obvious we weren't leaving anytime soon.

So I asked for another beer.

This was a *faux-paux*. They had run out.

Petite slipped one of the boys some money and he hopped onto his scooter to go buy more, just down the road. This made me feel bad for asking. But it was too late.

He returned just before we left, forty minutes later.

I grabbed a beer for the road, then banged my head on the way out again, enduring me to the small children. But it left the two elderly ladies wondering what kind of yo-yo Petite had married. One of them had passed around a sweetcake concoction she had cooked, a specialty of Hue. Wishing only to respond to the kindness, I had trotted out to the van and brought in my last partially melted Hershey With Almonds. A specialty of the USA. When I presented it, she pretended she didn't understand, and I ended up putting it on the table after she refused to touch it.

Later, I figured she must have thought it condescending to hand out candy bars like a GI rolling through the ville in the back of a troop truck.

Another unintended social error.

On the way to the cemetery, Uncle explained to Petite how important it was to hand over the money to the eldest family member. She would then dole it out. That was supposed to be the proper drill.

We crossed the Saigon River upstream of the city. It looked like the Mississippi. I wondered if they had any small rivers in Vietnam.

Petite's parents' cemetery was in a dusty field. A five o'clock sun beat down. Swarms of locals descended, as we made our way to the gravesite.

Uncle had purchased flowers and incense along the road. He took over, saying he was going to handle this and appointed one from the crowd to dust off the two graves.

A man, standing close by, said to me, "You Numbah One."

"You Numbah Two," I answered.

By my side, two little kids repeated over and over, "You give me money!"

I ignored them. We bowed before each grave.

Uncle planted pungent incense sticks into the dirt at each grave, a traditional Buddhist ceremony to honor ancestors.

As we walked back to the van, the one who had cleaned up the grave was screaming at Uncle, "You Numbah Ten! You fucking Numbah Ten!" Then a virulent spatter of Vietnamese.

Uncle appeared only slightly ruffled. It occurred to me that Uncle might have given the guy a less than generous tip.

Back in the van, Minh fired up the engine with the man still outside, ranting away.

Uncle slipped 10,000 through the parted window.

The little kids still eyed me, chanting, "You give me money," as we rolled away.

On the way back into Saigon, I managed to interrupt Uncle long enough to get a word with Petite. I was telling her what a klutz I had been for requesting a second beer back in Hoc Mon at the relatives' house.

Petite snorted. She said that they had had plenty of beer to start with. We were late. They had downed most of it by the time we got there. The reason it took forty minutes to get more was that the boy was tipsy and had run his scooter into a tree on the way back.

Fortunately, she said, he had only minor injuries.

In the back seat, I crossed my legs, wondering...

Was I going to be clueless the whole trip, or what?

"AMERICAN DREAM"

The name *Sai Gon* was a Viet corruption of the Khmer word for "kapok tree forest." In the sixteenth century dense forest occupied the stable ground north of a marshy swampland that extended to the ocean. Three rivers surrounded this land, with access to the South China Sea. The Khmer established a garrison in the seventeenth century after the fishing village began to attract an assortment of foreign traders.

In 1772 the Tay Son Rebellion forced the Nguyen family south to Saigon, where future emperor Gia Long relocated the capital. He walled the town. It remained the royal administrative center for the country's breadbasket after the capital was moved to Hue at the end of the rebellion three decades later.

In 1861 the French seized the town and made it capital of Cochinchina. It was the French who gave Saigon its legendary charm. In the 1930s Somerset Maughan described it as being like a "little provincial town in the south of France... a blithe and smiling little place."

The Japanese army occupied the city during World War II. By 1954 Saigon had become an Asian metropolis with a naughty reputation. In Cholon district, the Binh Xuyen river gang openly ran elaborate brothels, casinos, and opium dens. Their partners were French generals, as well as the deposed monarch Bao Ninh. Anti-colonial Vietnamese assassinated Frenchmen in the streets with pistol shots to the stomach - this method chosen for its lingering and painful death.

One particularly infamous brothel that I had read about was known as The Hall of Mirrors.

The street was thick with an opium smell. I reached for the door at the Hall of Mirrors, but it opened by itself. I stumbled in to find a fattened dwarf, who shut it tight again; pointing me to the Nubian maiden with glistening ebony breasts whom would escort me to the Menu Room.

"Would your preference be Asian, Caucasian? Perhaps fruit of the Nile, such as myself?" she asked in impeccable French.

I understood every word she said, and this did not seem unusual. There were a thousand choices here for a tepid evening such as this.

One by one, they lazily began to emerge through red velvet curtains at the far end of the Menu Room.

I heard a loud tapping in the hotel room. The air-conditioner was set at 65 degrees and I was on my stomach, sprawled over the bed at the Rex. Eyes stuffy but almost awake.

Damn those new thyroid pills!

Thought I heard another noise, at the door this time. No?

I closed my eyes again. Not asleep, merely resting, when the Devils appeared. Grotesque faces on an endless background of dark inner space.

A Demon's mustache suddenly melted away. His entire face then heated and bubbled, slowly vaporizing in anguished contortion.

Female creatures now howled, "MEE-EE, MEE-EE," with pitched squeals, like monkeys in a jungle.

Am I supposed to be scared? I thought.

Not asleep, I wanted to keep it going, actively imploring God at this point, so that the freak show somehow continued with bizarre visions I had never encountered before. Aberrant visages floating about, which did not seem human, yet I knew they were.

I stayed prone and stiff, my eyes shut.

Then a rumbling outside the door again.

The mind-show stopped, like one might switch off a porch light. Off the bed in a daze, I unbolted the front door and stared down the hall in each direction.

Empty.

I could only assume we had picked up ghosts at Cu Chi.

Most of them had been napalmed.

"At the time of their first stay it was late August.

Between the jungle and the forest along a stream, rosa canina blossomed in the rain, whitened everywhere, its perfume filling the air, especially at night.

The lethargy brought on by smoking rosa canina spread from Kien's scout platoon huts through the entire regiment. It wasn't long before the political commissar ordered the units to stop using rosa canina, declaring it a banned substance.

Many of the soldiers talked about seeing groups of headless black Marines, carrying lanterns aloft, walking through in Indian file.

It was here, at the end of the dry season of '69, that the 27th Battalion had been surrounded and almost totally wiped out by the Americans. Troops in the fragmented companies tried to regroup, only to be blown out of their shelters again as they went mad, became disoriented, and threw themselves into nets of bullets, dying in the flaming inferno.

After that battle no one mentioned the 27th Battalion any more, though numerous souls of ghosts and devils were born in that deadly defeat. They were still loose, wandering in every corner and bush in the jungle, drifting along the stream, refusing to depart for the Other World.

From then on it was called the Jungle of Screaming Souls."

From **The Sorrow of War** by Bao Ninh

I put on my swim trunks and headed upstairs to the pool, where Petite was. Heretofore, we had done our swimming early in the morning, when we had shared the pool with a German couple. We had not talked to them.

It was a welcome relief to get out of the room, although it was steamy outside the air-conditioning. After proceeding to the far end of the rooftop terrace, I climbed a spiral staircase up to the very top. The view was superb, you could see the whole downtown.

Petite was across the way. The area was compact; three tables with umbrellas, a narrow pool, and loungers. It would have been crowded with fifteen people. Now holding only half that, it seemed a small private theater, of sorts, with its inexplicable Greek sculpture of pink stone on a wall by the bright blue water.

Petite was delivering some sort of sermon to a fellow sitting in the next chair over. His back was to me. Business-length hair. About 40 years old.

I admired the way he listened. Gentlemanly. Attentively, not slouched over the deck lounger.

Whatever she was talking about, it stopped when I walked up. Petite introduced me, "My husband Harry."

The fellow was blond, blandly handsome. English, it turned out. This was his first trip back since 1975. His father had been a corporate executive for British American Tobacco. He was raised in Saigon and had attended a Catholic high school for foreigners.

I asked if he remembered Tet in 1968.

He said he did. He recalled that the VC had offered a cease-fire of longer duration than was normal. Many of the ARVN soldiers had come back to celebrate the holiday with their families, although normally they weren't allowed in the city.

The Englishman said, "It was around midnight. I was in bed but not asleep, when I heard shooting noises. I figured it was only

New Year's fireworks. See, Saigon had been hardly touched by the fighting at that point. It simply did not occur to me, even then at the mid-point of the war, that the VC could attack the city."

By the early morning hours the VC had infiltrated District One, downtown.

He said, "I figured it out when the mortar fire started. Then Father came in the room and told us that, among other places, the VC were attacking the American Embassy, not far from where we lived. I can tell you it was shocking."

He told us that his father had moved the wife and kids out of the country after that. He himself had returned to Vietnam in the early 1970s to work for the British embassy in Saigon.

It was hot and humid out. I excused myself and jumped into the pool. He was a good guy, I figured, having brought along his Mum and sister on this visit.

After standing on my head in the deep end, I came up for air. A resonating American voice boomed from the other end.

The voice's owner had a deep tan, no particular accent, silver hair, mustache, and slight paunch, which indicated to me that he was approximately my age.

American businessman, I figured.

He was gabbing away about something to a young Finnish schoolteacher in a black bathing suit.

Petite was engrossed in a novel as I stepped out of the pool. The British man had departed.

It wasn't long before the American came over and invited us to sit at the table with him and his wife. She was an Asian woman, reading in the shade of an umbrella.

Her name was Mai, his Liam.

They lived in New Jersey. Mai was attractive, about the same age as Petite, and it turned out they were both born in Hue. Liam told me that this was his first trip back to Vietnam since his two tours with the Navy in '67 and '68 in the Mekong Delta.

I was glad to meet them. He was the first American I had talked to in Vietnam; and a veteran, as well. Liam explained how he had spent two weeks in Saigon when he was nineteen, on "basket leave" in 1967, before there was such a thing as R&R. The skyscrapers we could see from the terrace were definitely different.

No more Tu Do Street, although the Bumble Bee nightclub was still operating, he said, pointing it out across from the Rex. But he hadn't been there. Neither had I.

Petite and Mai were chatting in Vietnamese.

Regarding the Navy years, Liam said, "During my first tour over here in 1967, you could *never* have told me that we wouldn't win the war." Liam paused. "It was never the same after Tet in 1968," he said.

We started talking to the girls.

Petite had left Saigon for America in December 1967, only five weeks before the surprise offensive by the Communists.

Liam's wife Mai was not so fortunate.

She was in Hue, one of the worst places she could have been. The Northerners and VC got in and occupied the city for awhile. They left behind 2,800 civilian corpses in one mass grave, with 2,000 more missing. It became known as the Hue Massacre.

She said, "Harry, on Tet they came to where I lived in Hue. They pulled us all out of our house into the street. One of them started screaming at me, 'Where's your brothers? Where's your brothers?' Harry, my brothers were in hiding. Next, they took Mother and Father. And they shot them in the street. In front of me!... I escaped. That's why I still hate Communists."

Normally I might have come up with a witty *repartee*.

There was nothing I could say.

However, things quickly lightened up. We were laughing.

"I finally made it to America," Mai said.

Like most *Viet Kieu* I have known, Petite included, Mai was more than willing to testify on behalf of the American Dream. She did so at the table by the blue water pool atop the Rex Hotel that afternoon. I have often thought that most of them were more patriotic and appreciative of the United States than native Yanks.

As for the local Vietnamese, they saw the amount of cash that their relatives were lugging back to the country from overseas. Also, a sizeable portion of the economy, especially in the decade after the war, was the influx of American dollars in the form of family donations sent over to help out.

Nothing in Vietnam's history seemed to counteract the view that America was one huge money factory, rolling poor men into the assembly line at one end, and spitting out rich men at the other.

"FAMOUS ARTISTS"

I traveled to Vietnam in 1998 with certain opinions about the war that had been formed decades ago and never questioned. Foremost was the belief that most of the population in the South at that time had not cared which side would win the war, but simply wished to be left alone.

The first person I met who prompted me to reevaluate this oversimplification was Mai. Whereas indifference was likely the rule in the countryside, where the inhabitants were often caught between the VC at night and the Saigon forces during the day, I came to believe that the vast majority in the cities was anti-Communist.

Also I came to conclude that the endemic corruption, which so horrified and repulsed the American military and Western media and eventually the American public, did not have the same effect upon the Vietnamese themselves. They seemed to accept it as the normal procedure for government officials since time immemorial.

It was easy for anyone to be critical, especially in hindsight. But hidden in the torrent of American self-incrimination over the past three decades were several rather successful efforts by the U.S. on behalf of the Vietnamese people.

Among these were numerous aid programs and especially the invention of Super Rice by American researchers in the Philippines. Distribution of these seeds in the Mekong Delta, the country's "rice bowl," soon allowed for three crops a year, as well as improved yield. The additional crop was known as the "Honda" crop because so many farmers purchased scooters with the extra income.

Due to increased prosperity, by the time of the fall of Saigon in 1975, the rural population in the far south mostly supported the government. The NVA never waded into the delta at war's end. Only when ARVN units holding the territory were finally ordered to surrender by Big Minh did they do so.

I was on the rooftop terrace at the Rex the next day, feeling guilty about having so many unchecked items still on my checklist. The guidebook intimated that the War Crimes Museum was the best of them all. We had yet to visit either the art or the history museum. Things to do, and here I was, slacking off by the swimming pool.

It was Thursday. We had to leave for Nha Trang the following morning. I was thinking about how I had almost gotten a good night's sleep, for a change.

Liam walked up and sat down.

I asked if he had been to the War Crimes Museum.

He said, "Yeah, it's a crock of shit... But you ought to go to just to see the deformed fetuses they have in these glass jars. All kinds. I've never *seen* so many deformed fetuses before."

It was true you couldn't see those just anywhere. I acted suitably impressed, then crossed it off the list. We were headed out to dinner tonight with a renowned painter, which covered the artsy-craftsy stuff. I had read plenty of history and doubted I would see much of it at the history museum.

Liam seemed to be settling in for some R&R himself.

I asked him if he had been out to Cu Chi.

He said, "Let me tell you about Cu Chi, if you've got a minute."

I now had all afternoon.

"A friend of Mai's brother here in Saigon, Mr. Long, drove us out to Cu Chi. For the trip, he wore his BDUs; battle-dress uniform, tiger pants and all. I told him he had more balls n' me.

They, the other Vietnamese out there, were pointing and staring at him."

"A heavy scene, no doubt."

"Well, actually, neither of us felt any animosity. If anything surprised laughter. I had on my Vietnam Vet tee shirt - South Jersey Chapter. Vietnam on the back, with our old war zone designations. Mr. Long told me, 'I want *hard* to remember!' So I promised when I got back home I'd get him another pair of BDUs, boots size-six, and Airborne hat. I guess some of the South Vietnamese soldiers are starting to come out of the woodwork. Back here in town, Mai's brother showed me a place in Cholon district where they go to watch underground copies of *Platoon* and other U.S. Vietnam flicks. Costs about a quarter. He also showed me where to buy old ARVN patches under the counter."

I wondered, "What did the guide at Cu Chi think about Mr. Long?"

"Oh he thought Mr. Long was cool."

It turned out that Liam's English-speaking guide had been a former ARVN soldier. We had different guides.

I asked, "By the way, what the heck is up with that hokey firing range?"

Liam rolled his eyes. "Harry, I gotta tell you about the range..."

"Wait a minute," I said. "Did the guy who carried out the rifle tell you that you missed your first shot?"

Liam looked startled.

"Yeah!" he said. "And I nailed it!"

"Me, too!"

We high-fived.

"I picked the AK," Liam said. "Oh man... I ran into two guys from Australia at Cu Chi. Kind of young. Thirties. Full camo tops and pants, Ranger hats. Both took out M-16s and couldn't hit dick. But they spent hundreds of bucks between them, firing the things on automatic."

That might have been me, if the last shot hadn't jammed and given me time to think.

"You could almost *buy* one for that in San Diego."

"Jersey, too," he answered, his eyes drifting away.

A Vietnamese girl with gifted proportions in a black bikini walked past our table, returned our stares, and went about looking for someone. We were sure she was a working girl, she passed by the pool like a fashion model. Finally she took off, disappearing beyond the fan palms toward the elevators.

"She's looking for a guest before 8 o'clock," I said.

Liam laughed wickedly.

According to the rules, guests could not have their own guests in the rooms after 8 p.m.

However, the downstairs lounge at the Rex was open to the public with a separate street entrance. Around the evening cocktail hour, it seemed to be quite a gathering spot for unescorted women. I didn't know how strictly the rules were observed in actual practice by the hotel. But of course Liam and I weren't interested in that sort of thing.

He said, "Let me tell you about Hue."

Liam and Mai were near the end of their journey to Vietnam. They were to leave for the states on Tuesday. He told me Mai showed him the place where her parents had been shot in Hue. It left quite an impression on him. Made it more real, I supposed. They had traveled from Saigon to Hue by train. Liam liked it, the food and everything. Coming back, they took a tourist van.

"I thought we were going to die," he said. "Not just once, either!"

There were 14 people crunched into the thing. The driver thought he was Mario Andretti.

I was soon to learn that Highway One to Hue was hard travelling for three bumpy days even under the best of circumstances such as we had. What if all the seats had been filled in Minh the Driver's van? Liam's Mario Andretti had run a couple of truckers off the pavement.

It seemed a good idea to not scrimp on transportation cost.

"While I was in Hue," he said, "one evening at dusk, I met some of Mai's friends and relatives outside the city who were ex-ARVN. They also had on remnants of the old war uniforms. Jacket liners, and so forth. One of 'em told me, 'No Communists here, only Como' as he held up an old PRIC 77 headset to show me. That explained his grasp of English. *Como* meant he was a Communications M.O.S."

I was surprised: ARVNs at Cu Chi. Guys dressed up in the woods with PRIC 77s.

What next?

I got to the hotel room to find Petite back from visiting one of her famous artist friends, who had picked her up in a chauffeur-driven car. He had married well.

Tonight we were going to have dinner with another famous artist, one who supposedly wasn't into money. These two famous artists were old buddies with Petite's brother who now lived in the U.S., the third famous artist. That is, they had all been close friends in bygone days. Now they were not.

Petite had expended a good deal of effort trying to contact them. She went into a number of art galleries to ask about them, receiving several frosty responses, as well as positive ones.

In one shop, Petite asked the proprietor, "Who are the famous artists these days?"

The proprietor replied, "Anyone who's dead."

Working artists were everywhere we went in the country.

The Vietnamese had a beautiful gift for color. Many of the paintings were very good, some of them great.

My favorites were traditional black or red lacquers.

For some reason, I don't know whether it was the humidity or the natural elements needed for the paint, but Petite's brother had explained that it was impossible to create these lacquers in the states. Certain seeds were needed to create the reds, the blues, the other colors. Ground abalone shells were often mixed into the paint, producing a pleasing shine and texture. I favored works in which the subjects were ghost-like, otherworldly, exaggerated as if they were creatures from another dimension.

For me, black lacquer gave the background a certain mystery.

That night at dinner Petite introduced us to the famous artist who claimed he didn't care about money. He had a white goatee and long shiny hair, also white, and sat at the table's head. To his left, Mai and Liam. To his right, Petite and I. The artist spoke limited English.

Liam had garnered his attention, explaining that he had been down in the Mekong Delta during the war. I heard Liam say something, then utter, *"Rock Yaw!"*

The old artist's eyes brightened.

"Ah, Rach Gia!" he said.

I had no clue, as usual.

He had taken us to a great spot. Another artist friend, a woman, owned it. I didn't know if she was famous or not. Fine yellow paintings lined the dining room, like something out of Dune, and a Chopin piece provided the background music. An adjoining outdoor nightclub could be seen through the windows.

The artist's son happened to be there tonight with his band.

Petite asked, "Who are the famous artists nowadays?"

The artist said, "The same ones as in 1975. You know all of them!" He started laughing uproariously.

Mai asked him something in Vietnamese. He directed his attention to the two ladies.

Liam leaned toward me. "Mai and I traveled back to my old swift boat base in Cat Lo, down near Rach Gia. Across the street from the former main gate, the South China Seas Club was still there. Different clientele. Still offering beer and girls, though."

I asked, "How about the rest of the place, was it the same?"

"Yeah. The gate to the base had a different sign. The village was the same."

Liam explained that he was on a fifty-foot sounding boat during the war, with a crew of seven to nine. The mission was to map the inland waterways and coastal regions in the Mekong Delta. The last time this had been done was by the French in the 1870s.

"Did you ever get shot at on the river?" I asked.

"Yes. And we returned fire, especially in 1967 in the Rung Sat zone. That means 'River of Death.' I'm no hero but we did get a unit citation for the effort we displayed. That's what got us the two-week basket leave. Hey, Nineteen? That's how old I was."

Not old enough to legally drink at home.

The waiter scurried around the table, wondering if we would ever order food.

Liam and I hadn't looked at the menu.

"Beer here."

"Beer here," I seconded.

The artist decided that he would do the honors for everyone at the table. He ordered crab-asparagus soup, then clams, and steamed fish with mint, and tiger shrimp, and...

Petite stopped him.

She knew I was allergic to fish but I liked pork.

The waiter left the table. We all decided to order whatever

we wanted, which would take another thirty minutes to finalize. The artist did not seem pleased I had fouled up the pecking order with my peculiar eating habits.

I went with the chicken. Liam and Mai deferred to the artist. Petite was still undecided.

I asked our friend with the goatee, "Are you still doing lacquers?"

The famous artist lifted his nose. He proclaimed that lacquer was for tourists and it was the choice of "artists" interested only in monetary reward. He admitted to some small amount of lacquer work back in the 1970s, divulging that Petite's brother also had done some of it at that time. But for both it was "only because we need money," he said.

I felt sucker-punched. His black lacquer production that hung so prominently in our living room was my favorite of all the paintings in our home.

I decided not to let *him* know that.

The artist told everyone at the table that he wished to move to the U.S. as soon as possible. He admired the tranquility and orderliness of Southern California, he said. It was so much easier to work in that atmosphere. The chaos here was getting to him.

He had come by himself tonight and I thought I remembered Petite telling me he wasn't married.

I kidded him, "Well, are you going to meet some nice young American girls when you get over there?"

The face behind the white goatee turned cold.

He said, "My wife died just six months ago."

Silence.

I apologized profusely.

Fortunately at that moment son Bernardo entered the room. Bernardo was tall, over six-feet, with a short black goatee.

We all stood up, with the famous artist beaming. Yellow

paintings graced the background. White linen. Crimson roses. So lovely a sight, I wished I had brought the camera.

Bernardo, who resembled Sinbad the Sailor, played a mean saxophone, and did some of the vocals. After dinner, we sat in the garden area, side by side on cushions, listening to jazz over after-dinner drinks. Bernardo was at the front of the stage going through heavy riffs on his saxophone. Getting down.

Petite chatted lightly with the famous artist.

I looked at her and felt romantic, holding her tiny hand.

My girl!

We got back to the hotel. Liam, Mai, Petite, and I stepped into the elevator. It seemed that we had become close friends, at least as much as it was possible, in two short days.

Liam's voice wavered. He said, "Harry, I saw a poster at a bar when we were up in Hue. It said: *After A Hard Rain, The Sun Will Shine*... And you know... that's how I see Vietnam today."

I thought, *Indeed!*

We said goodbye to Liam and Mai in the elevator.

Petite and I got off.

I turned as the elevator door started to close.

Simultaneously Liam and I gave each other one last inevitable, everlasting all-purpose, go-anywhere Peace Sign.

"RAU MUONG SAO TOI

The first four hours on the way to Nha Trang, the land was flat, much the same as around Saigon. I was quickly bored and engrossed myself in a novel. It wasn't uncomfortably hot in the air-conditioning with morning temperatures.

At noon we rolled off Highway One at Phan Thiet onto a road by the river. Minh pulled us into the parking lot for a restaurant. Across the river was a scenic pagoda.

Accompanied by children and a grizzled woman, a blind man with flowing hair hustled from across the road to greet us.

After five days in Saigon, I would have been surprised if he hadn't done that.

Petite readied the petty cash.

Soon we were seated at a dining table perched above the river. Minh kept insisting that we did not have to invite him to lunch. The $45 a day included his meals. Also, it was the custom in Vietnam not to eat with the hired help.

"I'm not Vietnamese," I said.

I had a lot riding on Minh the Driver. Before the journey, it was obvious that we would be around him for one week. Neither of us knew him. He was not a relative. For better or worse, the driver had been slated to be a middle-class prototype for this book before I ever met him. The plan was to draw him out, little by little. Get him to tell me what he really thought. I figured that this could be a delicate process in a society with a Communist government.

Petite would be my translator, and partner-in-crime, because Minh spoke as much English as I did Vietnamese: A solid ten-word base from which all communication must trickle.

Food arrived at the table, looking tasty; more than I could say for the fare at most countryside restaurants in China. In fact, there were some greens, like baby asparagus, sautéed in oil and garlic buds. More than "tasty."

Delicious. I loved garlic.

I asked Petite about the dish.

She said the dish was named *Rau Muong Sao Toi*.

It was not served much in San Diego. The greens, *Rau Muong*, were not readily available in the U.S. Petite was happy that I liked the broiled shrimp, as well. She had been worried about the complaints she thought she would hear from Mr. Hamburger on this trip.

Mr. Hamburger liked it! Even though we were far from Saigon, with its cheese omelets, French bread, pizza, ice cream, onion soup, Australian T-bone, and Petard a la Orange.

Rau Muong was the real thing.

It was now going so well, I decided to risk my first loaded question. I said to Petite, "Ask Minh what nationalities, if any, have given him the most problems in his four years as a driver?"

I supposed he would say the French, maybe the Germans.

Petite started laughing.

"Viet Kieu... Nguoi My," he had said.

Foreign Vietnamese and Americans. *Viet Kieu* were the most demanding, but it was a group of Americans who had gotten him into the most trouble. He said it happened at Cam Ranh Bay. The old U.S base, now filled with Russian navy ships, was totally off-limits. The Americans had been stationed there during the war.

They got Minh to drive to the area so they could take pictures, but the Vietnamese shore patrol stopped them. There was a heated argument; the Americans acting like they still owned the place. Minh was scared shitless the police would take his van, his livelihood. He was responsible. He was the driver.

The navy policemen finally let the Americans keep their cameras, after they tore up all the film.

Everything turned out okay. He was still Minh the Driver.

As we were getting up to leave the restaurant, Minh the Driver changed his mind. He said he had forgotten. Koreans were the worst. By far the worst.

Back in the van, Petite told me that *Rau Muong* was the what real people ate; those in the fields whom I referred to as "The Cone Hats." *Rau Muong* and rice were all they could afford on a dollar a day salary.

I told Petite and Minh that I planned to order a batch at every meal. They both thought that was funny. I supposed it was as if a foreigner came over and sampled American fare, including the rib-eyes, the smoked salmon, the pizza, the burgers and milk shakes, then announced that Collard Greens was his favorite dish of all.

The stretch of Highway One between Phan Thiet and Ca Na started out flat and dusty, with dragon-fruit plantings on both sides of the road. The fruit looked like an oversized pink hand-grenade. Once peeled, it was similar to a sweet pear with black seeds.

A rugged set of dry mountains loomed out the window.

Saigon did not have those. I was ready for some picture postcard stuff, but this stretch looked like Baja California. This was where we flew over on the way to Saigon. It was here, as we were making good time speeding along that I missed the taking the best snapshot of the trip.

A bend in the highway. Rockpile mountains. 95 degrees inside the van. Four women with bamboo cone hats bicycling in single file, perfectly spaced, each dressed in a white *ao dai* with a different pastel top.

Reddish pink. Light purple. Turquoise. Tangerine.

What color against the sandy backdrop! A Vietnamese gift.

We passed by. They looked somehow cooler than I was, although they were outdoors pedaling hard in the afternoon sun while I was in the so-called "air-conditioning." Cone hats were breezier than my baseball cap. Air filtered through the bamboo strips on a cone hat. According to Minh, there was no feminine connotation to wearing one, but most of the people I saw with them were women.

Along the road, we sped by a group of people whose headwear jerked my eyes around. Ethnic Cham, according to Petite. It was the only place we saw along the coast where indigenous peoples lived. Normally tribal people were in the highlands. Petite said that in general the Vietnamese looked down on all of them.

South of Ca Na, we came around a Baja-like curve. Below appeared a clean, deserted sandy beach, where a mountain shot down into the turquoise shallows of the South China Sea. We followed the road carved into its steep decline, and turned inland. The ocean disappeared behind. No pictures of that beach. No stroll on the idyllic sand, no swim in the clear waters.

It was hot. Late afternoon. Still, we beat it to Nha Trang.

Minh stayed busy up in front, driving and trying to improve his language skills at the same time. What English he could speak was almost undecipherable. The driver was too close to fifty-years-old, that age when it was hard to learn something new.

As for myself, I had already forgotten the Vietnamese for "Greens Sautéed in Oil and Garlic." All of four hours since lunch.

Petite tried to help him with practical stuff. To quit saying, "You go to bathroom now!" Or, "You eat now!" His verbatim transfer of Vietnamese into English. She taught him a few Western courtesies as well.

Minh replied, "Thank you. Please."

Just another ill-fated effort as far as I was concerned. I had refused to participate, until he asked Petite how to indicate anger in English.

Quickly off my back on the padded seat, I raised and shouted over the road noise: "Say **I am pissed off!**"

Petite made sure there were no further lessons from the peanut gallery.

Minh repeated, *"I am pissed off. I am pissed off. I am pissed off,"* in a desperate attempt to remember, as he nearly drifted off the highway. Face contorted. Visibly concentrating.

Naturally we never heard him utter it again.

At the town of Cam Ranh we stopped for gas.

It was 5 p.m. Stretching outside, I heard a voice on a loudspeaker from across the highway. Petite said it was someone delivering the news.

More Five O' Clock Follies.

Russian sailors were now stationed at the former Cam Ranh Bay base, about ten miles from the gas station where we were. Minh said they were not disliked. They generally kept to themselves.

When Petite got back, he started up the van.

I said in pigeon Vietnamese, *"Minh, di a Cam Ranh* Base. Take pictures of Russkis!"

I held my camera up with a wild-eyed look.

A nervous giggle up front.

He peeled out. We were off in a flash.

From Cam Ranh to Nha Trang, the road turned due north. The heat dropped to about ninety degrees, a different climate zone. The scenery was "postcard ready." We had finally entered the land of expectations.

Tropical paradise: Bright green mountains, coconut palms, languid turquoise sea. Good R&R Country.

I needed it after Saigon.

"THE RIVER"

Minh the Driver switched on the headlights about an hour before we got to Nha Trang. He recommended the Hai Yen Hotel, saying that it was "on the beach." I had picked out Vien Dong from the guidebook.

That one required a walk to the sand, he said.

I didn't care. The Vien Dong had a swimming pool.

Paging back to the hotel section once again, I found a city map, which showed that neither one was *on* the beach. Hai Yen *"played second fiddle to the nearby Vien Dong,"* according to the **Rough Guide**.

Minh collected a commission of some sort wherever we stayed, but the hotel's deal was not as lucrative for the driver if it was not prearranged. About eight p.m. we checked into the Vien Dong. We were not responsible for Minh's lodging. He drove off while we were busy negotiating for the standard discounts. The government owned every hotel we stayed at in Vietnam, including the Rex. If you stayed longer than one night, you paid lower than the stated rate, usually 20% off for three to five nights.

Petite and I hurried out to the pool, first thing. The pool was constructed with bush-league technology. No shallow end, difficult hand braces to lift yourself out. But after eleven hours on the road, the water felt great. We then had dinner poolside at the hotel restaurant.

Back in the room after a long day, I tried to get to sleep.

Petite read a book in bed, as she usually did for an hour or so before turning off the lights.

I had almost drifted into Nirvana. The telephone rang at ten p.m. I thought the calls would stop when we left Saigon.

Petite picked it up.

"Hello," she said.

I kept my eyes shut.

Then she asked loudly in English, "*River?* What river?" She said, "You mean?... I met you at a river?"

Was someone messing with my little girl?

"The hell is *that?*" I demanded, now awake.

Suddenly Petite laughed loudly, a unique sort of cackle.

She said that the "River" was actually our *Driver,* Minh, on the other end. Trying to practice his English.

"Alo, theese Mean the river!" he kept saying over and over.

"Minh The River" was born.

I shared the opinion of others who had been to Vietnam and came away thinking that Nha Trang would be the most pleasant place to live. It seemed to be as the Mexican Riviera was fifty years ago. There were no modern sport fishing boats around. No fiber-glass sailboats, either. No marinas, per se.

Nha Trang had a huge harbor filled with traditional blue and red-trimmed wooden vessels, serving as homes for the fishermen and their families. These boats had small motors to push them at a modest pace.

Long white sand beaches, clear blue water, and coral reefs were all about the area. The number of islands in the bay gave it a charming feel. There was still a perpetual haze; the same heavy air we encountered all over South Vietnam. I suspected it was a permanent feature. I cannot imagine the place without it; so unlike California's clear piercing glare.

West of the bay, the river split into dual channels forming the estuaries seen from the hills above. The highlands often came right up from the sea.

The downside to Nha Trang was that there was not a lot to do so far as nightlife. Only one Kleenex-box, luxury hotel existed, with rooms at $200 and up, a joint venture between the government and Bong-Bong Marcos, son of Ferdinand and Imelda of the Philippines. It wasn't listed in the guidebook because it opened after 1996.

Most Nha Trang tourists were French or other Continentals; types that wouldn't be caught dead paying those prices.

On Saturday morning Minh The River joined us for breakfast. What he had called about the night before was to tell us that Vien Dong had a dormitory room where drivers stayed for free, so he was right down the hall from us.

At breakfast we decided to stay in Nha Trang for three nights instead of the two originally planned. Minh's description of what would await us on a trip up Highway 9 to Khe Sanh left me deciding not to do it. Except for a concrete slab, Khe Sanh did not exist anymore, he said. Round trip would be ten hours driving time. My rear end still ached from yesterday's trip. Minh said there was no jungle up there, rather it was rocky and dusty. Most of all, windy.

I scratched Khe Sanh, its Central Highlands, the view of Laos, and the Ho Chi Minh Trail, which allowed an extra day here. Kurtz would have to wait. And I had conveniently forgotten about drinking any snake blood by this time.

Petite and I walked to the beach, passing through the grounds of the Hai Yen Hotel; the one Minh originally touted. Co-incidentally, Petite recognized it as the hotel where she stayed in 1993. She said it was much cheaper than ours was.

Ours was $35 a night.

We came out of a parking lot onto Tran Phu boulevard.

According to the **Rough Guide**, the locals still told stories about "*cyclo races the Americans once held along this wide, palm-lined cornich.*"

A cyclo was a three-wheeled cycle with a seat in front; a pedicab. As we crossed the boulevard, I envisioned young Marines on R&R; feisty, full of fun, pedaling furiously and dripping the sweat of honest competitive toil.

A drapery of trees and tall grass covered the view toward the ocean. We traipsed through an outdoor restaurant's patio toward a set of steps.

Hello!... White sand beaches, and clean to boot.

We rented an open hut with two loungers for $1.40.

The sea was very still and colored turquoise. Clear visibility, about 78 degrees water temperature. The foliage at the edge of the sand was luxurious. We were the first customers to arrive that morning, which meant that each one of the vendors dropped by to give us a pitch. Petite talked to a few, but we didn't buy anything.

Each one asked, "Maybe later?"

By mid Saturday morning the beach was busier but not crowded. I decided to get a rub down. It was a three-dollar deal. The woman claimed she had emerged from intensive government schooling, trained in the secrets of the Fine Art of Massage.

"*Oui, oui,*" I said earnestly.

Ten minutes later, her cupped hands making obscene noises slamming off blubber, she obsessively hand-whipped my back with cutting blows like it was caning hour in Singapore.

Then she halted suddenly.

I was relieved until I felt something grab my leg and start to yank a patch of hair. I turned around and looked.

A father had carried over Baby to see The Gorilla up close.

Touch it. Grab a souvenir, as well.

I glared at the infant.

The baby went, "*Wheeeeee*!"

A thrilled look from his beady eyes.

Glad his old man hadn't given the kid a cattle prod.

The masseuse now ordered me onto my back, and she vigorously slapped my head about, seeming to enjoy every second of it. Sandy hands scratched the facial skin like little wetted straps.

This seemed to last forever.

Cheeks afire, still I refused to call for quarter.

Name, rank. Serial-number only.

Petite thought it was hilarious for me to pay someone else three dollars to beat me up.

"You crazy foreigners!" she said, shaking her head.

After a day at the beach, we took off for a tour of the town at four p.m. Minh the River said he knew all the good spots.

We crossed a bridge over the harbor. Bright blue fishing boats to one side. Exotic rocks jutting from the bay. Just over the far side of the bridge, we turned into Po Nagar, the site of a collection of ancient Cham towers.

Beggars and salesgirls and saleswomen swarmed around the van. Petite and I got out. I felt like Bruce Willis at a Planet Hollywood opening night. A bedraggled pensioner latched onto my arm. A lot of her teeth were missing and she wanted a donation. We made our way to the entrance, her cone hat knocking at my side.

A teen-age girl had set her sights on my wife, and joined us in climbing the stairs to the hilltop where the towers were. The girl alternatively spoke French and English, while pushing a set of postcards in front of Petite that showed exactly what we were about to see. At the top of the stairs, Petite said, "Maybe later."

Standing outside the first small shrine we came to, I spotted a likely place in the shade for a cigarette break. I secured a seat and took a load off Fanny.

A skinny fellow came up. In English, he said, "I am here to tell you what to do."

Petite and I turned to one another.

I said, "Very interesting."

Immediately he directed me to lift my butt off the revered ceremonial altar that provided rain for the rice paddies.

Glancing down through crossed legs, I saw that my Nike had turned a burned-out joss stick to smithereens.

"So sorry," I said, jumping up.

The gentleman who was here to tell me what to do looked to the sky ominously. Not a cloud in sight.

Petite and I took off around the hilltop, which afforded a panoramic view of the surrounding area including the harbor entrance, the type of place where the Spanish used to place their fortresses in the Caribbean. Some of the best real estate in town. The Cham towers were constructed with long rectangular bricks. There were four Hindu shrines of different sizes in a clearing on the hill. All were shaped and decorated like lotuses, the same as our playing card symbol for spades. Plants and vines grew out of the bricks, giving it a Mayan flavor, but the architecture was distinctly Asian, such as the layered three-dimensional lotus sculptures set into the brickwork.

I left my Nikes on the steps outside and entered the main temple barefooted. Cosmic candles twinkled inside a short corridor. Coming up behind two ladies who were bowing deeply, I saw a female wooden idol in her radiant yellow dress. Smoke from the numerous incense sticks was thick and pungent. Bowls on the altar were filled with ripe tropical fruit.

Marlon Brando might dig this, I figured.

The temple's colorful ceramic tiles attracted me, glistening in the heavy interior moisture like they were alive and sweating. A red one, a beige one, a brown, a green. And to one side of the altar, an elephant statue that looked somehow human.

The ladies lighted still more joss sticks, placed them between their palms and bowed again, chanting all the while.

This was no museum, but an active shrine.

Old-time religion.

Walking back down the stairs from the hilltop, the postcard girl met us halfway.

"No thanks," I said.

"You say, 'Maybe later.' Why not?" she asked.

"We don't need any postcards. I took photos."

I pointed to my camera to prove that I wasn't just making it up.

"But these aren't the same," she sniffled.

When we got to the bottom, she stumbled away looking like she would throw herself over the nearest cliff because we didn't buy anything.

The old pensioner scuttled over, grabbed my arm once again, and started agitating about something in Vietnamese.

I couldn't remember borrowing money from her, at least in this lifetime.

She gesticulated all the way to the van.

As we escaped out of the parking lot, I glanced back.

She held up a single wrinkled index finger, flashing the aged digit in my direction. It wasn't the friendly sign, either.

That did it. I had spun around in Saigon only days before to see a beggar on Le Loi Street spit at me just as I passed by. I had simply ignored it then.

I got the witch's full attention then lifted my forefinger, crooking it to one eye.

She saw it!

Dr. Peabody once referred to this as "A most ancient Western curse, known as *The Evil Eye.*" If I had pulled this stunt on an old bag in Italy or Greece, it might have resulted in a coronary on the spot.

No such luck here. Oblivious to my Old World Double-Whammy, the woman shrilled something in a more venomous manner than before, still socking it to me a hundred-percent as we sped away.

There were few beggars in the North. In the South, there was little rhyme or reason as to whom Petite and I handed out money. Generally we gave deformed or blind people something. Humorous situations abounded in this atmosphere. We both got tired of it, too. I guess it pretty much depended on what type of mood we were in at a given time.

Next, Minh drove us a short distance to Hon Chong promontory with its idyllic, Greek-like view: Water and rocks, a mountain across the bay on the far shore, its three rocky ridges forming a lifelike outline of a woman resting on her back.

Worth a visit.

It was here that I bought myself a cone hat for 5,000 dong, or thirty-five cents.

Back at the beach area, we arrived at the Sailing Club, just down from our hotel. It was a great place to eat, especially the Italian menu, and one of the few we went to in Vietnam that paid any attention to decor. Perfect rows of coconut palms stood along the beach by the dining tables. There were bonfire parties in front of the Sailing Club on weekend nights, according to the waiter.

The sun went down as we dined. Soon I glanced over at the horizon and noticed an unimaginably large neon sign illuminating the far reaches of the bay. But there was no hotel on the outer islands as far as I knew. Then I looked more closely.

Slowly rising was a blood-red, full moon; so huge, it seemed like the sun. So bright, it first appeared as neon across the water.

Petite and I decided to take the short hike back to the hotel after dinner. Bouncing in the dark along the sidewalk on Tran Phu Boulevard, a thought occurred to me when I saw a cyclo driver pedaling by.

Actually it was more a revelation than just a thought.

Those heralded cyclo races during the war?

Those strapping young Marines I had imagined, pouring sweat in honest competitive toil?

They were the riders, not the horses.

Not the "rivers," as they pronounced it in Vietnam.

"MAMA LINH

Nha Trang was barely touched during the war. Even then, it was a tourist town. The CIA directed anti-terrorist programs from there, but the American presence was less than in most areas of South Vietnam. Communist forces did not attack the city.

At harbor side on Sunday morning, Petite pointed out a ten-pound block of ice as it was dragged melting over a concrete road covered with the type of dirt and grime that looked tubercular. I hoped they weren't shipping that batch to our hotel.

It was perfectly sunny out. We hopped aboard the boat for a day's cruise to five different islands. I thought many of the other passengers boarding looked like Japanese tourists. Two women nicely dressed in heels brought along carry-on bags. As it turned out, the "Japanese" were Vietnamese, that is the women with various wardrobes for the day. Both were honeymooners.

I had on a fishing tee shirt, shorts, and swimsuit underneath. Petite wore a one-piece under her shorts and top.

The idea of getting dressed up in high heels for outdoor recreation seemed peculiarly old fashioned.

Another "Japanese" fellow tourist turned out to be a *Viet Kieu* from Canada. He had come home to get married. On the boat, he spent a lot of time chatting with two unescorted French girls, while his beautiful bride looked on nervously.

As we put out of the harbor a couple of sleepy Vietnamese teen-age girls, flopped across the benches next to us, asked the captain if the boat could please come back an hour early this afternoon. They had a train to catch.

Petite and I got a chuckle out of that.

85

The water offshore turned four different colors of blue-green. Gradients, which fish run along, were more visible than in our part of the Pacific.

We came to an island and anchored in 30 feet of water outside a reef. The island itself looked like Hawaii. Tropo. The view in other direction, out to the ocean, was Mediterranean: rocky, granite islands sticking out of the water here and there. Only occasional stretches of sand appeared on any of the five islands we were to visit.

At this first stop we dove in for an hour's snorkeling. I was the only one in the group of fifteen who refused the floatation ring. But then I was the only one fat enough to float *au natural.*

The corals were okay. Water visibility was about the same as Cozumel. I saw a moray eel stick out his head from under a rock. There were a lot of small tropical fish.

The Vietnamese thought the water was bone chilling at 78 degrees.

Back aboard on the way to the next island, the captain of the vessel pulled out a handy guitar. He started into an Elvis song. The passengers got into the act, clapping and laughing. He then sang a song each in French, Vietnamese, and English, to "promote international friendship." It was corny but fun. Elvis rocked away on his gee-tar, shaking like the King himself, butchering the English. I'm sure he did the same thing with his French song, as the two French girls started laughing harder than the rest of us during that one.

But the entertainment on our boat was tame stuff, indeed.

At a lunch stop at the second island we anchored across from Mama Linh's two boats which were strapped together.

Loudspeakers blasted out "Around The Bend" by Creedence. Her group of lusty Euros and Aussies boogied away, sloshing beer on the top deck of her party boat. Directing the action was Mama Linh herself: Trim. A youthful fifty-year-old in tight camouflaged tiger pants and a black Ranger hat. She held a microphone, thrusting her pelvis on the dance floor.

Her throaty voice carried over the water above the music: *"You don't drink no beer, you don't get none of Momma's lunch, honey!"*

On our boat, Captain Elvis folded down the bright blue benches we had been sitting on to form a wooden dining table.

Out came the grub from a small kitchen in the stern.

The Captain came by for drink orders, the only additional expense to the $7 price of the trip.

I requested a beer without ice. Many Asians preferred to pour it into a glass with ice cubes, which kept it colder. Until just recently, I had adopted this custom.

The fare was local seafood cooked on board. Afterwards, bundles of fresh fruit. Everyone seemed to enjoy the meal.

When we pulled anchor, I glanced toward Mama Linh's crew. The top decks were deserted and no music was heard.

Thirty minutes later, we pulled up to island number three.

Again Elvis got everyone but me into flotation rings.

"It's Happy Hour!" he shouted.

He jumped into the sea with a cooler strapped to a float. Everyone followed, except the two teenagers who wanted to get back early. They never went in the water, and slept on the benches ninety percent of the time.

Once in the water, it was hard to slurp my complimentary cup of sweet red wine and stay afloat without a flotation device. However, the other passengers seemed suitably impressed with my dog-paddling-while-imbibing routine. Two of them I met at this Happy Hour in the drink were a married couple from South Africa, who lived in Toronto. They said it was a bad situation at home in Africa. Many Whites were emigrating.

I heard Petite shout over to say that the Canadian *Viet Kieu* was about to light up a huge joint.

I swam over, seriously doubting it.

The tall, handsome fellow floated in his ring with a hand-rolled stogie in his mouth, the end still not pinched.

Captain Elvis did not appear to care, bobbing on a float, putting down wine.

I was still skeptical but not as much as before. It looked like the real thing.

"It's just tobacco," the man with the stogie laughed.

He lived in Toronto, too, but he didn't know the two South Africans.

"Where's your wife?" I asked.

He said, "On the boat, changing clothes," laughing again.

When we were back aboard, one of the French girls put her tee shirt on. I had noticed it on the cruise out: A yellow star on a red shirt, the same as the national flag.

I never saw a Vietnamese wearing one of those. I was curious if she had bought it as a political statement, or for some other reason. She wasn't the fashionable type - thick set.

On the next island was a sand beach, as well as an entrance gate where we paid to get in. When everyone bore left toward the beach, Petite and I took a right at the sidewalk and went off on our own. We passed a group of Vietnamese on a Sunday picnic back in the bush, who offered us beer and asked us to join the party. We thanked them and continued along the shore.

The sidewalk ended around a bend. Stepping into the water over the rocks, the ocean was calm as a bathtub, clear, and the temperature perfect. I bent over to the waterline with my camera. Petite's face reflected off a cobalt sea. Green mountains rose to the sky. Puffy fingers of clouds crept down the valleys.

Snap.

We strolled back to the sandy area past a row of rental beach huts.

"Where you from?" one of a group of kids asked, giggling, passing by.

"Vietnam!" I said, friendly as can be.

"Where you from?" she said again. Giggling some more, pointing, walking away, turning back to look.

Guess she didn't believe me.

Petite said they were pointing to my tee shirt. It had a bull dorado painted on the back trying to munch a flying fish. Before the trip, I had thought about going offshore to fish in Nha Trang, but there hadn't been a decent runabout in sight.

All the swimming made my ankle sore. I hobbled toward the dock, Petite leading the way. About halfway back along the sidewalk, we heard a tremendous commotion. Mama Linh's pair of boats were heading into the dock area, her speakers blasting the shore like the 88's once did to the Au Shau Valley.

The crowd of mostly Vietnamese tourists on land froze in their tracks, gaping as the boats slowly navigated to the cement pilings.

Coming from the arriving armada, I heard, *"... AFN Vietnam. This one's going out to Leroy in Da Nang First Marines. Gone slammin' today in the big bad smelly jungle. Whoa Lordy! I Heard It Through The Grapevine, Brudda Leroy!"*

"Damn," I told Petite, "The ol' gal must have recorded this stuff way back when... Un-bloody-real."

"Bet you wonder how I knew
'Bout yo plans
To make me blue..."

Mama Linh, the last of the Red Hots, slow twisted, almost dirty dancing with two bare-chested Euro studs as the boats eased up to the dock.

A Danish kid stumbled off in a daze and teetered about on the dock, beer in hand.

On the boat, Mama grabbed a microphone.

Pointing, she shouted at him, *"You no come back one hour, Mama leave you ass here!"*

Even from a healthy distance, it was apparent that she enjoyed this brand of theater, played to a captive audience of several hundred onshore.

Then I heard it.

"GO-OD *Morning, Vietnam!"*

The Oh-So-Familiar Voice of Robin Williams, as it coursed through the speakers on the boat.

The soundtrack from the movie.

"Hey Private Randy Myers, out there with Eleventh Cav, lookin' for pajamas in the paddies. Ever wonder how come Ho Chi Minh looks so much like Colonel Sanders?"

My face darted to others standing along the sidewalk.

The two Vietnamese teen-age girls had arisen, cleared their eyes, come ashore, and now had their eyes glued on Mama Linh with hypnotic stares.

They could not have looked more in awe if a space ship had just blown into town and popped the hatch in front of them.

"HOME OF THE BRAVE"

The following excerpt appeared as a column in the government's English language daily newspaper, *Viet Nam News*. Most of the youth I talked to seemed to concur with the sentiment expressed by author Nguyen Ngoc Huong.

"Sometimes I feel like asking my mother: 'Do you think it is fair that you always blame the mistakes you made on things which were outside your control, and yet my mistakes are always of my own doing?'

People of her generation always seem to blame the mistakes they may have made on factors such as the war, or the centrally planned economy, or the poor education system.

The younger generation, they say, have no such problems to face. Things are easier today and therefore there are no excuses for failure.

People of my generation, those born after 1975, often complain that they feel burdened by the weight of their parent's unrealistic expectations. They say that the older generation expects too much and are too unforgiving of young people's mistakes.

I myself do not feel the same kind of burden, but I do feel frequently that I have disappointed my mother in some way or other and that I have no way to restore the damage.

At university, my professors always compared our time with theirs. They would always blame their shortcomings on their lack of opportunities or the 'historical conditions' of the time. But I always suspected that this was too easy. Surely the older generation should not blame everything on such external factors. Surely they should accept some degree of personal responsibility.

Not long ago, I sat by chance in a class of 18-year-old girls. One of them wondered why her marks were so low. There was silence. Suddenly one girl, imitating a professor, replied, 'You know, we have had to suffer a lot. Two wars and stepping straight into a socialist economy before experiencing a capitalist one. Tell me how, under such conditions, you could have expected anything more?'

The girls burst out laughing. And I too felt like laughing because I had heard the same explanation used so many times by the older generation. Of course it was true, but I felt it was simply stating the obvious, akin to saying: 'We need oxygen to breathe.'

We are all aware of the past and, no doubt, we should not forget past glories as well as losses.

But we should learn about these things in an objective manner. We should be able to compare our time with theirs in a rational way. By living life with one's foot always stuck in the past, the older generation view today's with 'blinkers' on.

Our generation was brought up with clear identities. We were taught that we belonged to a nation famous for its bravery and its wealth of natural resources. I feel sure that nowhere in the world is national pride as strong as it is in Asia and in Viet Nam. I understand this pride and it is a necessary thing. But please, don't make that past unassailable. Don't make it inaccessible.

If everything our parent's generation did was perfect, then how can we possibly live up to such unattainable targets? The younger generation seems destined to disappoint.

To understand the spirit of the younger generation one has to accept that it is a generation like no other.

It is now time for this generation to take over the legacy of our predecessors and spearhead the country's economic and cultural development.

It is true young people today have many opportunities to better themselves through training or hard work. They have not had to suffer in the same way as their parents. And because they have not been confronted with death on a daily basis, they are not so traumatized by the memories of war. This is not to forget that this same younger generation has lived through another traumatic experience - extreme poverty.

Because of this shared experience, the younger generation is not afraid of hard work and young people are not afraid of overcoming obstacles. And at the same time they are not afraid of enjoying the fruits of their labour.

I have seen fellow students happily sign up for unskilled and frankly boring manual work to help support themselves through college. Others work as waiters or waitresses or even motorbike attendants.

I feel pride in my generation because it is a generation that has been able to adapt to the demands of a new age. As such, this younger generation should feel happy with its role in society and it should be aware of its own identity.

We have all been taught that 'where there's a will, there's a way.' The younger generation has that will, it has its own dynamics and it should be given its own chance to succeed without feeling hamstrung by the weight of unrealistic expectations.

I want to say to my mother, 'Your time was different from mine.'"

"THOMPSON, LANSDALE, ELLSBERG"

Daniel Ellsberg knew what he was talking about when he revealed that LBJ cranked up the war on purpose in 1964 by ordering the CIA to attack and provoke North Vietnam. This was to deceive Congress into passing the Gulf of Tonkin resolution, which would be the basis for expanding the war.

Ellsberg, not be confused with an idealist at the early stage of his diplomatic career, was one of the few people in the world at the time who knew the facts about what happened on that August night in the gulf. And Ellsberg was one of even fewer who knew the CIA had secretly been attacking the North on the two days preceding August 4, 1964.

Completing the equation was a haunting suggestion that the two U.S. destroyers comprising the "task force" involved on that day were in the area really to provide a couple of fat targets, against which the North was welcome to vent any anger it might have stored for transgressions imagined or otherwise. These attacks remained so secret that by the mid-1990s Robert McNamera would continue to describe them in his book as South Vietnamese attacks, although the South had nothing to do with them whatsoever.

But the scheme had worked. Unfortunately, 364 days after the "Tonkin incident," regular American ground troops put a village to the torch for the first time.

Ellsberg knew about the CIA attacks, as he had known much earlier in 1961 that if one were involved with Vietnam it was like being associated with the recent Cuban Bay of Pigs fiasco, in that it would ruin one's career. The kind of "perfect failure which ruined the careers of nearly anybody who had touched it," as

Ellsberg explained in 1998 during an interview at the Institute for International Studies, UC Berkeley.

Before 1961 there was Eisenhower. And there was Edward Lansdale, as his fellow CIA members saw him, holding the dike against the angry sea of Communist aggression, midwifing the Republic of South Vietnam. Executing the transition of the south from French to American influence, with his indispensable aid and advice, preventing Ho Chi Minh's takeover of the entire country. He bribed President Diem's domestic enemies. He organized the military struggle against the Binh Xuyen gang and he helped to rig the first election ever held in Vietnamese history, while directing an ongoing psywar "dirty tricks" efforts in both north and south.

Lansdale soon learned that though Diem was a proxy, he was not a puppet. Nevertheless, by the time Kennedy came along, the focus in Washington was on Cuba.

Nixon had called Kennedy soft on Communism during the 1960 election. It was a sensitive issue with the president. After the Bay of Pigs, money that had been going to nuclear war research became available and Kennedy directed some of this to South Vietnam. He himself was a World War II hero, his administration's fight against Communism had been less than rewarding thus far in Cuba, and he needed a winner.

According to Ellsberg, the secret dope on Vietnam was that everyone knew it was not winnable in the long run, but Kennedy went against this advice. Therefore, a case could be made that U.S. involvement with Cuba was an important factor in Kennedy's decision to commit to Vietnam. JFK said, "Vietnam is the place."

With his habitual smile, Lansdale realized when few of his countrymen did in 1965, that use of artillery against the villages was the most strategic of errors if one wanted to win the war. It went against everything he had counseled and in which he believed.

Author David Cornwell's view of the secret world was that

it mirrored a nation's subconscious, and to look at the missions of a country's intelligence services revealed its longings and anxieties.

In this respect, Lansdale will give future historians Freudian fits. Ed Lansdale's contemporaries ranged from Neil Sheehan, who dubbed him the "Father of South Vietnam," to Stanley Karnow, who passed him off as an overtouted, idealistic advertising man.

So it was Daniel Ellsberg through his intimate knowledge who would grant future historians the clearest look at the era.

As it was Hugh Clowers Thompson, Jr. who would serve to remind them what a real American hero was.

The field in Quang Ngai province was salted with sea water by the ARVN long ago and left to dry - dusty, dead already when shells from the American 105's landed at 7:27 on a Spring morning after Tet in 1968.

Americal Division intelligence said the villagers would be gone to market several miles away. They were not. And according to division intelligence, the 48th Local Force VC Battalion would be in the area. They were not. U.S. Army Intelligence in Saigon knew this. It was never clear why Saigon realized that the 48th was no more than a decimated group of between 30 to 100 soldiers who had limped to the mountains west of Quang Ngai to rebuild after Tet, while the field division commander for the Pinkville Operation assumed they were about to encounter 300 enemy soldiers.

The boys of Company C, average age twenty, were ready for this one. Orders were to burn the village and kill the livestock. At exactly 7:30, the artillery barrage stopped.

Three helicopters appeared over the field, machine guns pointed down, wasting the LZ that was now covered by a white phosphorus dust cloud.

One chopper swept to the ground. The lieutenant inside

yelled, "Let's go!"

First platoon and part of second platoon, the first lift, scrambled into defensive positions. To the right of the chopper a first platoon machinegun opened up. Tracers flew above a farmer, fleeing with his cattle. Suddenly an M-79 grenade launcher fired, hitting short of the farmer with its bomblets kicking more dust.

The first chopper took off. The pilot radioed the aero scout that the LZ was "cold."

The aero scout, a small bubble-top chopper, came in fast over the trees darting above Tu Cung hamlet, then it banked and returned for another pass. Its mission was to spot for the ground troops, as well as draw enemy fire.

From the LZ, the soldiers poured rockets into the western fringe of the collection of huts. Soon the troops were spreading out.

Carefully one old farmer raised his hands to show he had no weapon. He flipped back, a machine gun killing him instantly.

Twenty minutes on the ground. Charlie Company had its first "VC."

The second lift brought in third platoon and the remainder of second platoon.

Piloting the aero scout, Hugh Thompson radioed, "We got a couple running with weapons below." He dropped smoke, marking the spot where two men had just tossed the rifles they carried.

First squad of third platoon under Lt. Geoffrey La Cross took off away from Tu Cung to gather the arms.

One of the grunts from another squad in third platoon, a tall soldier from Chicago, suddenly fired an automatic blast from his M-16. A woman carrying a child scurried away at a distance through the bush, ducking beneath his aim.

Immediately he was reprimanded for firing toward where the first squad in his own platoon had gone, just beyond the woman and child.

Third platoon had been assigned cleanup.

First and second platoons began advancing into the hamlet abreast in a line, firing from the hip. Search. Destroy.

No hostile fire had appeared as they entered the center of Tu Cung, which was code-named "My Lai 4."

At this moment, shortly before 8:00 a.m., Company Captain Ernest Medina radioed from the hamlet: 15 VC killed.

The first big lie of the day.

Far out from an irrigation ditch that cut a semicircle forming the southeast border of the settlement, the aero scout carefully descended. Hugh Thompson, its 25-year-old pilot, guided her down with the help of crew chief Glen Andreotta. Lawrence Colburn, an eighteen-year-old gunner, steadied the M-60 machinegun sights on two unarmed Vietnamese men raising their hands below.

Thompson's radio communications were only with the gun ships above him, not with Americal troops on the ground. He radioed to Big Huey to come down and pick up the two suspects for interrogation. By the time the Huey landed, it was 8:30. Thompson and Andreotta decided to fly back to LZ Dottie to refuel.

He radioed the "Charlie Charlie" ship way above, where Lt. Col. Frank Barker, the task force commander, monitored the battle.

While Thompson refueled at LZ Dottie, Barker checked again with Captain Medina on the ground to find out how things were going. Medina now reported a body count of 84 VC.

Another lie. His body count by this time was far higher.

Not one an enemy soldier.

"In fact it was worse than a massacre. Too many of Medina's men were taking sordid pleasure in sadistic behavior. Several became 'double veterans,' GI slang for the dubious honor of raping a woman and then murdering her. Many women were raped and sodomized, mutilated, and had their vaginas ripped open

*with knives or bayonets. One woman was killed when the muzzle of a rifle barrel was inserted into her vagina and the trigger was pulled. Soldiers repeatedly stabbed their victims, cut off limbs, sometimes beheaded them. Some were scalped; others had their tongues cut out or their throats slit or both. Tommy Lee Moss saw Vietnamese place their hands together and bow to greet Americans; only to be beaten with fists and tortured, clubbed with rifles, and stabbed in the back with bayonets. Other victims were mutilated with the signature **C Company** or the shape of an ace of spades carved into the chest."*

From **Four Hours in My Lai**
by Michael Bilton & Kevin Sim

"I went to turn her over and there was a little baby with her that I had also killed. The baby's face was half gone. My mind just went. The training came to me and I just started killing. Old men, women, children, water buffaloes, everything. We were told to leave nothing standing."

Varnardo Simpson

"I noticed this one small boy had been shot in the foot. Part of the foot was torn off, he was walking toward a group of bodies looking for his mother. I put up a camera to my eye, I was going to take a photograph. I didn't notice a GI kneeling down next to me with his M-16 rifle pointed at the child. Then I suddenly heard the crack and through the viewfinder I saw this child flip over on top of the pile of bodies. The GI stood up and just walked away. No remorse. Nothing. The other soldiers had a cold reaction - they were staring off into space like it was an everyday thing."

Ronald Haeberle, Combat Photographer, Pinkville Operation

Thompson and the others in the aero scout were on the way back to LZ Dottie, when they flew over two dead VC just killed by a Huey gunship. The soldiers were about twenty years old, not in uniform, but carrying GI gear, an M-1 and a carbine fully loaded. Thompson dropped smoke to give the pick-up boys a read. These would be the only two VC casualties of the day. The VC cadres needed to leave behind but a few soldiers to control the villages and to harass the Americans.

After refueling Thompson took off for Tu Cung again. In a paddy outside the hamlet, he took the chopper over an injured woman sprawled in a field. Circling back, they marked her position with smoke. About to fly away, they saw the company commander, U.S. Army Captain Ernest Medina, walk up to her.

To the disbelief of all three men in the chopper, he nudged the woman with his foot, then shot her through the head with his service pistol.

Dipping low over the irrigation ditch, Thompson noticed bodies sprawled out. Furiously he put down the chopper. Beneath the downwash, he was now out of the Plexiglas cockpit. The air smelled like grass fires.

A husky army sergeant ran up to him.

Thompson asked if there was anything he could do for the people in the ditch.

The sergeant calmly answered, "Only way to help *them* is put 'em out of their misery."

Lt. William Calley, the first platoon's officer, two-tailed it over to the chopper.

Thompson asked, "What the hell's going on here, Lieutenant?" Fuming, shaking his arms at Calley.

The lieutenant told the chopper pilot that C Company, meaning himself, was in charge down here on the ground.

Frustrated, Thompson returned to the helicopter.

Everyone inside was jittery. As they lifted off, they witnessed the husky sergeant shooting people in the ditch below.

Thompson headed off to the northeast corner of the hamlet, where second platoon was because second platoon were notorious "gangbangers." Rapists.

Thompson had a vision. Nazi soldiers mowing down the local peasants beside a drab Russian ditch. His chopper buzzed a patch of trees and settled over a green field and a group of Vietnamese quickly darted into sight below them, scrambling across the green to a homemade bomb shelter across the meadow.

"Uh, oh!" said Andreotti.

From the woods appeared second platoon, in pursuit, bouncing along under the heavy equipment.

Thompson landed. Frantically he turned to Colburn, pointing at second platoon, telling the gunner that if any American started shooting: "Open up on 'em - Blow them away!"

Bewildered, Colburn had not expected that. He thought it crazy landing between the troop and villagers, anyway. But he quickly aimed the M-60 at the advancing GIs.

Thompson was already out of the chopper approaching Brooks, the platoon leader. Thompson got in the lieutenant's face. The enlisted men in second platoon pulled up, with Colburn's M-60 covering them.

Inside the chopper, Colburn was not at all sure he could pull the trigger if something happened. If he did pull it, everyone was going to get killed including himself, he figured.

Thompson shouted at Lt. Brooks that he would go get the people out of the shelter. He could do it by talking to them.

Brooks was frustrated too. He said, "Only way to do that is grenades."

Above the roar of the helicopter, Thompson told Brooks to stay put. "I'll get 'em out," the pilot said.

Thompson headed to the bunker. He delicately persuaded one of them to come out. Nine others followed. Everyone got out before second platoon blew the shelter.

Back at the chopper Thompson got on the radio, his voice choking, and called in an evacuation ship.

One of the pilots above questioned the request.

Thompson flew into a rage. He cursed, demanding help immediately. He said he had ordered his gunner to open up on second platoon if anyone tried to harm villagers.

The radio operator above heard this and realized what was happening. He called Charlie Charlie to get someone up there to tell the ground troops to cease firing.

Two large helicopters soon bounced into the clearing. Thompson escorted a couple of men, a couple of women, and six children into them. The choppers took off for the road to Quang Ngai City and let down the villagers, miles away in safety.

Thompson and crew had been on the ground for twenty minutes. In the air again, they were about to head back for LZ Dottie when Thompson flew them the opposite way, toward the ditch.

Andreotti shouted that he had seen something move.

Thompson landed the aero scout and manned the M-60, covering the other two as they got out. Blackened straw from the huts still floated in the air.

Andreotti eased his way into the ditch up to his waist in a pile of cadavers. Among the gassy smell, the blood and mangle, he noticed a single flash. Movement?

After shoving two bodies aside, he saw a three-year-old boy toward the bottom. Andreotti lifted out the child, waded back to the edge of the ditch, and passed him up to Colburn.

The boy was limp but completely untouched, alive. But in the chopper, the child went into shock, and lay across Andreotta's arms. They made a beeline for the ARVN hospital in Quang Ngai City, eight miles away, where they handed him over.

Because of the stop at the hospital they got to LZ Dottie late at 11:00 a.m. Thompson jumped out and threw his helmet to the ground. He reported what they had seen to Major Fred Watke, his company commander.

The Hueys were landing now, too. They confirmed the description of the massacre.

Watke rang up Lt. Col. Barker in Charlie Charlie.

Barker instructed the executive officer, Major Calhoun, who was flying just above the area, to "find out what is happening and get it stopped."

Shortly thereafter, Captain Medina radioed his three platoon leaders ordering them: "Stop the killing."

Before noon the brutish activity halted. Quiet fell on Tu Cung. The hamlet now embers, Charlie Company, some along the ditch only yards from the dead, sat down, popped C-Rations and settled into a hearty carbohydrate-filled lunch.

Chow time after Rockin' n' Rollin' in Pinkville.

"AMERICAN TAKEOVER"

The events described in the previous chapter were taken from the authoritative study, **Four Hours In My Lai**, by Bilton & Sim. If I could be King, I would make this book required reading in high school history classes. Toward the end of the semester, after all the hero stuff had been digested.

What was most interesting about the My Lai massacre was why it happened, given the Judeo-Christian mores that America taught and that most of us professed to espouse. The book explained why, and also followed up on the events afterwards. The military bombed the whole area to try to cover it up. The photographer who was quoted happened to be carrying his own camera, a Leica with color film, as well as his official military camera. He did not turn over his own film.

Afterwards, the troops started talking because they were bothered badly by what happened, and many had nightmares. The word got around in other infantry units about certain things that went on during Pinkville.

Sad to say, however, that My Lai was not a one-time event. On the same day, March 16, 1968, Bravo Company, of the same Americal battle group, killed 90 of 100 villagers in Co Luy, a few miles away on the coast in a separate incident. While they were at it in Co Luy, Bravo Company raped the women, too.

The Army was fortunate when the news of My Lai finally broke in the worldwide media months after the fact. The story broke about the same time as the American landing on the moon. The American news hierarchy refused to give the story much play until it became the prime international focus by its own weight; and by what it said about the reality of war versus the official line.

The South Vietnamese government claimed that the massacre was nothing but propaganda, though it knew the truth.

The U.S. Army carefully termed it an "incident," rather than a massacre. They had a fall guy, too, in Lt. William Calley. The Army's defense consisted of its numerous written directives prohibiting such behavior in the battlefield. These were used to shield the upper echelon and to avoid any linkage between Charlie Company's actions in My Lai and such tactical concepts as search and destroy, body counts, free fire zones, etc.

However, at the time I went to the My Lai Memorial at Tu Cung, I had not read the book. I knew very little about what happened there, one day after the Ides of March 1968.

We bumped along Highway One several hours out of Nha Trang. I had one eye out the window on freshly harvested rice drying on the pavement, the other on my guidebook.

The countryside between Nha Trang and Hoi An was gorgeous and lush. I had been trying to read about My Lai in the guidebook and look out the window at the same time. Our game plan was undecided. Petite's father was born in Quang Ngai City. No one seemed to have an address for the house where was he was born, so we decided not to drive around the city when we got there.

I asked Minh the River how far My Lai was from Quang Ngai City.

He told me it was only twelve klicks, and he knew how to get there.

I wasn't completely sold on going out of our way for what was sure to be another humbling experience, and started in on the article again. "My Lai" was the American military code name for the area. The massacre was at a place called Tu Cung, designated

"My Lai 4," one of several hamlets which made up Son My village. It started to describe the events of March 16, 1968...

Hold it.

"What is today's date?" I asked Petite.

She said, "March Sixteenth."

The 30th anniversary of My Lai.

We had to go.

At the gate, it was 4:55 p.m., still plenty of light. The lady at the ticket counter said they were holding it open later than usual today. There was a big ceremony in the morning. It had broken up about noon, she said.

I had read about two Americans named Thompson and Colburn who were staying at the Rex the same time we were.

Petite had seen Thompson. There had been a "Colonel's Conference" at the hotel the last two days we were there.

I happened upon one of the former colonels once, and it certainly cured me. Coming around a corner on the fifth floor, I witnessed an uptight-looking character in Dockers and a golf shirt pace stressfully beside the door to the banquet room. He looked like every chief financial officer I'd ever had at the time of the Big Forecast. I thought, "These guys never change."

At the gate to My Lai, a woman in the ticket booth was trying to overcharge us. I saw Petite and Minh the River both giving her hell about it. Kids by the gate started pointing at me.

Minh remained outside with the van. He'd been to the memorial before. He pointed out a village clinic not far from the site, which had been donated by U.S. Navy veterans. His European clients all came here, he said.

I steadied myself for the ordeal as we marched in.

Hey, *I* didn't kill anybody.

Which was true, as far as it went. At the tender age of

106

twenty-one, I knocked a German citizen over the head with a full bottle of ice-cold beer in downtown Berlin on Kufurstendamm Strasse. So as far as my own military experience during the time of the My Lai massacre, I could not truthfully say I had not attempted to do harm to a civilian myself. Anyway...

Petite and I came to a small bridge walkway passing over a lovely stream about six feet wide, covered with lilies. At the far end of the central path we were taking was a large statute. It was hard not to be self-conscious. I felt that every Vietnamese walking toward us was staring at us in contempt. My *Surf Mexico* tee shirt turned out to be a less clever disguise than I figured it would be.

I took a lot of pictures: Bullet holes in palm trees. Mortuary-like memorials marking each torched hut. An imposing white stone statue depicting a family, with stands of flowers used in the memorial ceremony still in front of it.

After that, we stopped a woman so Petite could ask in Vietnamese where the ditch with the bodies had been. I'd read about it in the **Rough Guide**.

The lady didn't smile back. However, she helped us by pointing to an area about sixty yards past the statue.

The irrigation ditch was a bit steeper and deeper than I had imagined. It was carrying slow water.

At the opposite side of the park, the western edge, was where the Americans had landed. Now, in the cooler part of the day, four women in cone hats were cutting golden rice in what had been the old LZ. The area around was woods interspersed with fields about two hundred yards wide, running in clearings between the trees. Each field, divided into five or six long areas, had rotating crops in the different strips. I later learned that Quang Ngai province was now among the most prosperous farming regions in the country.

I was disappointed that the memorial to My Lai was not as

I had preconceived it, a working village with a few memorial signs. This was a production: A huge stone sculpture and two permanent buildings erected on the site. For the Communists, the massacre was the greatest tool one could imagine. They had taken advantage of the opportunity.

We went into the museum, which backed up to the old landing zone west of the park. I was a little defensive by this point. There was a pictorial history of the province, then a photo of a helicopter landing on a dusty LZ which bore no resemblance to the field I had just seen.

The next picture was of GIs torching a hut with Zippo lighters.

"Another proud moment in American history," I sighed.

We came to a section which showed the follow-up congressional investigation and the court martial proceedings. A photo of Lt. William Calley. I had heard somewhere that he was such a stupid asshole, one of his own men had decided to put a frag on him at the first available opportunity.

Staring at Calley's self-confident photograph taken when he was living with his girlfriend under "house arrest," I thought I could see why. But I figured they could have gotten him if they really wanted to before the platoon ever moved into the village.

Seeing Calley's smirk brought back the worst of my fear, loathing, and distrust of officers.

At the time I figured wrongly that if the men had only fragged Calley before My Lai, this never would have happened.

While perusing a group of framed pictures showing the congressional investigator, it occurred to me that the museum pointed to the magnitude of the event here as something out of the ordinary. There were no aspersions evident at the memorial that this type of activity had happened a lot.

I knew that there were no such North Vietnamese

government investigations or court martials for the massacre at Hue.

I came upon pictures of villagers who had been slaughtered that day. These were sad. The final body count was 347 at Tu Cung, with the only U.S. casualty a soldier who shot himself in the foot to avoid the carnage.

The last section of the photo gallery was dedicated to Hugh Thompson, Lawrence Colburn, and Glen Andreotta. There were excerpts from **Four Hours In My Lai**. The plaque said that Glen Andreotta had been killed in the war shortly afterwards.

When we stepped out of the museum I saw a red banner with yellow Vietnamese writing. It hung over the front entrance.

Curiously, Petite had difficulty translating it.

Always Engrain Hatred Deep In Your Heart For The American Takeover Of The Country

It was ironic. I had come to believe that the Americans were never in as much control as they thought they were. I figured the Communists knew that as well.

Then I wondered if Hugh Thompson or Colburn had noticed the sign among the hoopla this morning during the ceremony. Later I saw a *Sixty Minutes* segment, which had covered the story on location earlier in the day, but it never mentioned or showed the sign. Was the banner hanging during the ceremonies?

Why wasn't it mentioned during the telecast?

As we strolled back along the lane toward the entrance, it now seemed that the Vietnamese happening by were not the least bit disdainful anymore. They looked frightened, as we passed by. It occurred to me, they might be seeing me as some killer on the road coming back to visit the old stomping rounds. It was the only thing I could figure.

We climbed back into the van. Minh the River had figured it would take us about thirty minutes to see everything, but we had spent over an hour. We still had another two hours to go to Hoi An.

Kicking dust, Minh gunned the van out of the parking lot.

Five hundred yards down the road it got a bit congested, entering a ville. Minh sat on his horn trying to scurry through. In twilight he turned sharply, hitting the brakes.

Tires squealed.

I was pulled forward in the back seat.

A boy on a bicycle careened away.

God, I thought nervously, *They'd drag us out and lynch us if he ran over somebody.*

Wrong place. Wrong time!

At 4:00 a.m. on Thanksgiving 1998, eight months after the journey, I was outdoors before dawn's early light staring at our new redwood deck, which seemed to extend, albeit in two levels, as far as the eye could reach.

I was editing this piece in my mind, at the same time wondering if I could actually afford to live in this country any longer.

Palau must be cheaper. What could she do with a thatched hut?

I got up from the lounger and briskly strolled to the outer edge of this fallen redwood forest that stretched out toward the horizon. Like General Patton, I surveyed the grand scene below – elbows out, hands clenched at the hips.

I recalled something clearly that an Aussie friend, John, once told me when we were in Sydney several years ago.

John said, "Bloody Americans 'er brainwashed."

And I had agreed, though he had not expected that.

Many Americans would protest, saying *"We've got CNN! NBC, CBS, ABC, MSNBC. The Times, The Post…"*

Sure. We had all of those.

But they served it up with too much slant for my taste. I believed that point-of-view was necessary for a novel, but it was poor form in reporting news. BBC, as well as some others of the overseas media, seemed to reflect less bias in reporting. BBC focused on world events, as opposed to the stare-at-oneself-in-the-mirror approach.

The 1960s vintage media had quickly hopped on the bandwagon as it chugged out of the station for the great adventure in Southeast Asia. Among the cheerleaders had been the American TV networks, magazines and newspapers; less so the wire services with their international clients. *TIME* changed its slant on the war so suddenly that I remembered thinking when it happened at the time: "Gee, now they don't like the war. That's not what they were saying two months ago." Two months earlier, this was 1968, *TIME* had been reporting the conflict World War II style. *"The gallant platoon…"*

Now thirty years later in 1998, we seemed to have come full circle. The gist of the *Sixty Minutes* segment regarding My Lai's anniversary was one of reconciliation between America and Vietnam. The segment highlighted the return of Thompson and Colburn to the hamlet. The agenda for this particular piece seemed to be to heal old war wounds. So the fact of a banner proclaiming "Always to hate the American Takeover" would simply not…

"Fit" was how they usually put it.

According to Johnny, my Oz compatriot, this way-too-successful manipulation of American public opinion began many moons ago.

"THE PARTY OF THE PEOPLE"

On the road to the ancient port town, Hoi An, we were hyper after the day on the highway, and after My Lai, and after the near accident. I decided to strike while the iron was sizzling. Petite translated the questions being hurled from the rear of the bus.

It happened that Minh had grown up in the city of Da Nang, less than an hour up the road from Hoi An. He would spend tonight with his family after he dropped us off at our hotel. We were now in the area of Vietnam he called home.

"Were you with the ARVN during the war, Minh?" I asked, knowing that he wasn't.

He giggled. "I hide," he said, before Petite translated.

According to Minh, people in Da Nang were very anti-Communist. He claimed he did not know one person in Da Nang who ever worked for them.

I said, "I saw pictures of people in Saigon who helped the VC."

Petite translated for me. It was dark outside. Minh had the headlights full blast but they were dim by American standards. Shadowy figures on bicycles shared the highway. He took his eyes off the road for a couple of seconds. We sped along and Minh turned, looking at me, explaining to Petite in Vietnamese.

She said, "He says that the ones in Saigon who supported the VC are sorry they ever did that now."

After 1975 Minh the River made his way to Saigon. He was there illegally for years and finally saved enough to bribe someone to get legal, then started his driver job five years ago.

I asked him, "What did you do when the military drafted

soldiers for Cambodia?"

"I hide," he said again.

In response to another of my inquiries, he informed me that corruption was far worse under Communism than it had been before.

I expressed dismay.

Petite agreed with Minh. She had paid no bribes to get her student visa to go the U.S. in 1967.

Petite asked Minh about his family.

He was married with three children. He took pictures out of his wallet. A handsome family. Then he started telling us how much it cost to send the kids to school.

"Wait a minute," I said. "It *costs* to go to school?"

Indeed.

It depended on the grade the student was in: $60 for primary school, $100 a year for high school.

Minh said it was a lot of money in the countryside, where the average wage was less than one dollar per day. Therefore, half the children in rural areas could not afford to attend school.

I couldn't believe what I was hearing.

It was a socialist country, wasn't it?

"Was school free when you grew up?" I asked Petite.

She replied, "Of course."

It was free when Minh grew up, too. He said that the tuition system had been in effect in Vietnam for about the past ten years.

I considered this lack of equal educational opportunity more disgusting than, and a sadder fact than any of the war atrocities I had heard about by either side. To be fair, I didn't know how accurate his fifty-percent number was. But after all, in any society there should be free public education.

The current practice knowingly condemned a significant portion of the country's youth to lifelong poverty.

The Party of The People.
Yo?
Come again?

"HOI AN"

We got to the Hoi An Hotel at 8 p.m., and asked for the price list. The prices ranged from $30 to $100 per night. As soon as Minh the River waved goodbye and took off for Da Nang, the desk clerk informed us that the cheapest room now available was $60. The cleaning girl told us the next morning that there were plenty of $30 rooms empty.

Hoi An was the most touristy place we visited in Vietnam. That is, touristy for Vietnam. It wasn't Orlando. We stayed at the most expensive hotel in town.

That night we wandered three blocks into the center of town and had dinner at *Faifoo* restaurant. We arrived late, just before nine p.m. Three young Frenchmen sat at a table by the street side entrance. I had picked out the place because the guidebook mentioned that *Faifoo* served guacamole.

Our waitress was a friendly girl who studied English in her high school class during the day, though she looked about twelve years old. She brought out her school notes to ask a question about something she didn't understand.

I answered her question, then thumbed back a page in the notebook. I noticed where her teacher had corrected one line on the preceding page: "**No. Correct form is: 'I *sends* the package to him.'**"

"This one's wrong. It should be: I *send* the package."

The girl stared at the sentence in horror.

"But my teacher wrote it!" she said.

I got the impression that if it appeared on the next test, she was going to answer "I sends." To hell with what I said.

The girl disappeared and returned with a bowl of surprisingly tasty guacamole. No tortilla chips, of course, but I didn't need any. I nearly inhaled the porcelain bowl along with the chow and ordered another beer as well as a second portion of guacamole.

With the second serving, the girl brought out an extensive inventory of post cards, as well as four British coins that some unprincipled Limey had foisted on her. She managed a crocodile tear, explaining how the Pommy woman had paid for postcards with the coins, fooling the poor girl into thinking they were worth a small fortune.

"These coins all have a picture of the Queen on them," she pointed out. They were worth "beaucoup bucks."

"Americans once suffered under the yoke of English imperialism and its tricky ways, too," I told her.

But we did not need postcards. Coins, either.

She looked emotionally distraught, putting it all neatly back into her pack. A great salesman.

I felt a slight tinge of remorse for not buying anything.

Before we left, she sat down with us and told us she was sixteen years old. She had an uncle in the USA, she couldn't remember exactly where. Also, she had a "boy friend" in America. She said she would be moving to the U.S. in two years when she got out of high school. Then she would marry her American boy friend when she was 25 years old.

The little girl said it all very confidently.

I thought, *What a marvelous planner she is!*

The next morning we walked around the several blocks of Hoi An's historic center. The guidebook said it was a favorite for tourists. A cryptic comment I found on the Net before we left San Diego stated, *"All is not as it seems in Hoi An."*

This would be true for anyplace - Jasper, Texas, or Beaver Creek, Oregon. Nevertheless, it did intrigue me before we left.

Hoi An's landmark feature was a Japanese bridge, covered as in the Middle Ages, and pink, dating from the sixteenth century. The tourist attractions were primarily along Tran Phu Street: Several Chinese Assembly Halls, pagodas, and merchant's homes. The assembly halls were in such good condition, a rarity in Vietnam, that it was possible they had been almost completely refurbished. Aside from that, the mysterious "all is not as it seems" allure did not live up to its billing for me.

Hoi An was good for taking photographs, worth a morning's visit, but perhaps because I was not a devotee of Chinese architecture, the place was uninspiring. "Quaint" and "cute," yes, but it did not look real. As usual, we saw no other American tourists. Mostly French and German.

Particularly disappointing was the so-called "European Quarter." I had expected something akin to Macao, the ex-Portuguese colony off the South China coast, with its bawdy New Orleans-type architecture. No such luck. The Euro Quarter was almost uniformly Asian, but with a balcony or two.

Hoi An seemed like a Disneyland, of sorts. The real deal for that sort of thing turned up later in Hue.

We walked the few short blocks back to the hotel in extreme heat and humidity.

As usual, people were coming up to us and hounding us, or merely staring, or asking where we were from, or begging, or trying to sell us something. Now, instead of being pleasant, I walked along with a stone face, dripping sweat, silently ignoring human contact as if other people did not exist.

The downside to traveling in Asia was that it could turn you into someone you didn't want to be.

Minh the River was waiting in the lobby when we got back.

Checkout time was noon. A thin aging porter wearing a tattered army hat followed Petite upstairs to get our bags.

I proceeded to the front desk.

As usual, we had checked in our dollars and our passports at the front desk. An officious woman behind the counter began to prepare our bill. She noted that we had used one bottle of water from the mini-bar in the room. 1500 dong.

The old porter staggered into the lobby under several tons of luggages, our two bags. I could scarcely lift them myself. The woman behind the counter tore off a sheet of computer paper, announcing that I owed her $60 for the room.

I asked for the envelope out of the safe. It contained my American money. Then I reached in my wallet, pulled out 1500 dong for the mini-bar bill, and put it on the counter top.

She glanced down at the counter.

"Sixty dollars!" she said.

"This is for the water," I told her in a quiet voice, motioning toward the safe.

She jerked the statement of charges back, turned it around, circled the amount, and thrust the bill at me.

"Sixty Dollars U.S.!" she demanded.

I guessed she thought I was trying to pull a fast one.

Then she shrieked, "Sixty dollars *now!*"

I leaned over the counter.

"Get my money out of the safe, Asshole. Then I'll pay your goddamn sixty dollars!"

It was an embarrassing incident; the only confrontation I had in one of the hotels. I felt bad about it almost immediately. Perhaps she did too.

The porter managed to drag our bags outside. He loaded them into the van without any of us offering to help.

I had 5000 dong in hand for his tip.

"Cam on," I said, nodding, meaning "Thank you." I reached out to give him the money.

He shook his head, bowing slightly and smiling, backing away, indicating with his hands that no tip would be accepted.

It was the first and only time that happened during our trip.

I tried to guess why. Either he never accepted tips, or he thought I was such a creep that he was putting me down, or he thought the woman at the desk was such a jerk that he wouldn't take the money.

To this day, I have wondered which it was.

"LAST MARINE"

After a week in Okinawa waiting for assignment, my brother-in-law, Marine 1st Lt. Jake Steele, landed at the airfield south of Da Nang in October, 1970.

He had been briefed to use caution when driving outside American bases in Vietnam, that even small children would sometimes toss grenades or homemade bombs into vehicles. He would be riding in an open jeep into Da Nang city, then north to Red Beach, where the First Marine Division was snuggled against the mountains on both sides of Highway One, before the road climbed to Hai Van pass.

The jeep carried a sawed-off shotgun strapped to the driver's side. Jake noticed it, and at the same time his nose caught the smell of rotted rice.

Riding into Da Nang, they passed an open sewer.

Holy Cow!

The driver swung north along a blacktop road by the Han River. He followed it into town with the flow of bicycles and motorbikes, as well as autos, trucks, and busses belching black carbon.

Jake wondered, *How the hell could you ever tell the bad guys in this place?*

It seemed impossible.

Along a shady city street, the Marine driver pointed out the river and the French-style buildings facing it. A peculiar scent of herbs passed over the jeep, where people sat outside on the sidewalk at a group of different stands having soup for breakfast. The jeep came to a stop light at an intersection with a wide street.

Suddenly people on the street crowded around them while the jeep waited for the traffic light. A boy yelled out something in broken English.

Want to buy?

Jake looked away.

The driver gunned it, and took a left on the green light. They drove along just missing all sorts of cyclists, who seemed to know exactly when to dart out of the way. It made Jake nervous.

Before long, they were at the edge of town and a jagged stretch of peaks such as he had never seen in Tennessee or Arkansas dominated the view ahead. The blacktop road followed a set of railroad tracks. Two bridges, one for the rails, crossed a river. In the bay to the left were anchored sailing dhows. Huge butterfly shrimp nets were set into the shallows. Behind it all, a towering green range where fingers of white clouds spilled into the upper valleys.

Puff the Magic Dragon, in the Land of Honalei.

Past the bridge, a set of Hueys flew in formation over them.

POMP POMP POMP

The driver shouted to him over the noise.

"Dogpatch," he said, pointing to the civilian settlement that ran through the middle of the area where the Marine base was.

After several blocks of small shops, then past a Vietnamese cemetery, they turned left. Along bleached-white salt flats, they stopped at the guard post.

Jake sneezed. He looked around warily.

Inside the perimeter, an empty armored personnel carrier raced by kicking up dust as the jeep pulled over at the First Division reception center.

At the center he hooked up with a buddy who had been with him since basic training and through OCS. His buddy had just been assigned to a unit out in the boonies.

Jake had pulled Da Nang, right here at First Division. A supply unit.

He was glad about his own assignment.

Cam O was the Vietnamese name for what the Marines called "Red Beach." It was long. A white sand beach running a half-mile south to the river mouth. There on March 8, 1965, the 9th Marine Expeditionary Battalion came ashore and was formally greeted by the local authorities.

At this time, the Marines had been in Vietnam for three years, since 1962, but only as advisors.

The USMC was the first service to get heavily involved in Vietnam. The Corps' biggest ground offensive of the entire war was Operation Starlight in August 1965, an early period of the conflict. Third Marine Division was stationed north on the DMV and east into the mountains to Laos and Cambodia. By 1968, the entire area from Da Nang, to Hue, to the DMZ, was known as "Leatherneck Square."

From January to March 1968, Khe Sanh firebase was surrounded and besieged by the NVA. During that time, the Marines were also routing the enemy out of Hue, the only city occupied by the North during the Tet Offensive.

12,983 Marines were killed in action from 1961-1975, according to an Internet site, MarineLINK.

However, Neil Sheehan, in **A Bright Shining Lie**, put the number at 14,691. *"Three times as many as had died in Korea, a weighty loss in lives, a loss that weighed more heavily than the 24,511 Marines who had been lost during World War II."*

Sheehan's next sentence was, *"Brute Krulack knew, before most of these Marines in Vietnam had died, that all of them were to die in vain."*

As with Lansdale and John Paul Vann, but with few others

in the American military establishment elite, General Victor Krulack believed that our success in Vietnam would rest in the hands of the Vietnamese people.

It was early in the conflict when Krulack presented his case to President Johnson as such:

"Krulack explained that the strategy of pacification and social and economic reform was the only way to succeed. Attrition was peripheral to the real struggle.

'Big-unit fighting with Main Force Viet Cong and NVA could move to another planet today, and we still would not have won the war because the Vietnamese people are the prize,' he said."

Next, General Krulack was given a pat on the back and shown the Oval Office door.

The Bob MacNamera-William Westmoreland gang had taken over.

What a pair.

With friends like that, small wonder Johnson retired early to the Pedernales River and to an early death, wondering how he could have messed it up so badly.

By the time Jake arrived it had been Tricky Dicky's war for years.

By the time Jake landed, Nixon was busily floating rumors through Henry Kissinger that he was only a Gin-and-Tonic away from obliterating Hanoi. From punching the nuclear button. And Henry luckily had been there to stop him in the nick of time. This was known around the White House as the "Madman Theory": Nixon's attempt to scare North Vietnam to the negotiating table.

By the time Jake got there, Nixon's "De-Americanization" program was in full swing. MacNamera and "Westy" had long since departed. Total American dead dropped from approximately 12,000 in 1969, to 6,000 in 1970, to 3,000 in 1971.

Mr. Nixon was in the position of trying to negotiate while withdrawing. Not a mean trick, as they say; and one in which his vast political skills proved useful.

Little did Jake Steele know in October when he landed that he would be the last Marine on the boat out of Da Nang, only eight months later in the Summer.

His tour of duty in Vietnam afforded him little time to see the country, except by helicopter when they used to fly over the mountains. There was still plenty of fighting when he got there. On a visit to First Marine headquarters one day he happened across the place where they stored the incoming body bags, with its lingering acrid smell.

At times, he visited a Vietnamese orphanage off base.

Most of all, he hated the job. From his description, it was much like my own work in the army. Yes, you stayed alive, but it was mind-numbingly stupid and boring.

There were occasional attacks on the base: Rockets, as well as interdiction and harassment fire and such from the NVA. On one starry night the machine gunners at the western perimeter repulsed a determined sapper team. Jake took photos of the bodies left hanging in the wire the next morning.

Whenever they were attacked, Marines within the perimeter at Da Nang would "call up the jets" and watch the show from below.

But by the time summer rolled around in 1971, Jake was more afraid of the black Marines in his own unit than of the NVA. He had been platoon leader of African-Americans before, but not like the ones in Vietnam, where black power and drugs were in full force. Several times, the officers caught prostitutes sneaking among the outer perimeter and partying in the foxholes, which afforded the base its protection. This made Jake uneasy, as well as the fact that everyone carried weapons. Fragging was in vogue. Southern white officers such as Jake seemed to be prime targets.

He and I have talked about this. Separately, we arrived at the same conclusion: Vietnam was a lower-class war.

Both of us Southern fraternity boys had few peers who were in any military service at that time; much less did we know many of those who went to Vietnam. Bill Clinton was not alone.

By 1970, a phenomenon caused by the government's draft policy and by the war put the inmates more or less in charge of the asylum known as the American military. This was true even in Berlin. It was sort of a selective refusal to follow orders.

In reference to the U.S. Army in Vietnam, Neil Sheehan wrote, *"It was an army in which men escaped into marijuana and heroin and other men died because their comrades were 'stoned' on these drugs that profited the Chinese traffickers and the Saigon generals. It was an Army whose units in the field were on the edge of mutiny, whose soldiers rebelled against the senselessness of their sacrifice by assassinating officers and noncoms in 'accidental' shootings and 'fraggings' with grenades."*

For the last month, Jake was transferred to the engineers: The "take it down/clean it up" boys. His own men in supply had shipped out back to the states. He wrapped it up by supervising the hand over of USMC equipment to the ARVN.

Seabees tore apart everything that the ARVN didn't need.

His engineer battalion was the last USMC unit to leave the area.

Finally, under a blue sky over Monkey Mountain, Jake was the last Marine to step onto the boat when it left the green waters of Da Nang harbor.

With all due respect to Vietnam, he never wanted to see the place again.

"DA NANG"

We stayed at the Bach Dang Hotel on Bach Dang Street, which fronted the river along the route that Jake took. As elsewhere, the people who worked at the smaller hotels were friendlier, more helpful. The Bach Dang cost $40 a night for a large art-deco style room. An airy paved square in the midst of the hotel grounds gave it an out-of-place Italian flavor.

On Wednesday morning, Minh the River drove us north to Cam O Beach. I wanted to take pictures for Jake, since he didn't plan to come back himself.

The ville, which had been called "Dogpatch" by the Marines, looked ordinary. We passed through it, turned to the right off Highway One onto a dirt road, and ended up just south of a giant cement factory almost on the beach.

Petite and I got out and talked to some women who lived there in a group of shacks. They pointed out a long cement pier and told us it was a fuel depot the Marines built. They were happy to see us two Americans, as were all the people we met in this area.

Petite and I walked together along "Red Beach." The sand was white-white, but the water a little murky. A beautiful pine forest lay back beyond the strand, and it was there I found some old "fighting holes" dug into the ground.

When we got back to the van, Minh the River told us he knew of a better beach just down the road.

We crossed back over the bridge toward Da Nang, and took a left shortly. This place was not in any of the guidebooks that I read. It was called *Thuy Yen*. It had the same type sand as Cam O, but the water was cleaner, more blue. There was a small restaurant and fresh-water showers. We were the only people on the beach, which afforded a spectacular view of the mountains, the bay, and the picturesque sailing dhows, which comprised the local fishing fleet.

On the way from Hoi An when we were south of Da Nang the previous day, we had stopped off at China Beach figuring to have a swim. But it was windy. The beach didn't look that great to me, anyway, so we smoked a cigarette and left. Thuy Yen was much better than China Beach. Excepting Nha Trang, it was the best one we went to in Vietnam. We soaked up the rays, strolled around, showered off, and had lunch by the sea.

Minh drove us back into Da Nang and stopped in front of a grassy site with a yellowed orange building surrounded by a wall, close to the Han River.

The Cham Museum.

Petite and I encountered a four-foot tall professor on the front steps of the museum. He offered to guide us for a nominal fee and we happily accepted. Though his English was indecipherable, he seemed a character. And from the appearance of the sculptures standing at the entrance to the museum, the Champa in these parts were into the "funkadelic" look.

A huge stone parrot beak and an elephant body.

The place was open-air, to boot.

A lot of it was Indian, like Po Nagar, with the attendant sexual depictions. Elephants were heavily represented. I was attracted not so much to a statue of a Hindu goddess as to its shiny bronze sign. It was one of the few in the museum with an English translation.

While leaning close to read the engraving, I saw that:

This style tend to express queer animals such as lion, elephants, sea monsters, dragons, etc.

Our nutty professor guide thought my jokes were hilarious.

Therefore it was irrelevant whether I could understand him or not. I supposed he figured that Petite was Japanese at first because he seemed so surprised she could speak Vietnamese.

She started to pose in front of a bulky sculpture, mimicking the female dancers on it perpetually frozen in mid-squat.

The professor clapped his hands enthusiastically. Now he started speaking rapid French, claiming he knew it much better than English.

Petite took a snapshot of me standing next to the happy elephant god. Gandalf or something; a good-luck god. Then we thanked the professor for the tour.

I asked him, "What religion are you?"

He said proudly, "I am a Theist."

I asked, "Is that Hindu or maybe an ancient Champa cult?"

"I am a *Theist*!" he repeated. Slightly perturbed.

Whatever it was it sounded mystic to me.

"He's *an atheist,*" Petite explained.

Across the street from the museum, we found the van parked and locked. Minh the River was nowhere in sight.

A middle-aged white woman walked up to me and asked, "Sir, can we take this van to our hotel?"

"No, it's ours," I told her.

That was, of course, if I could find the driver.

"Ah, the driver is *ofer* there," she said, pointing.

I recognized Minh standing against a wall forty yards down the way. Apparently she had already talked to him, and it was all right with him if it was okay with me. She explained that Minh would drop us off first, and apologized for the miscommunication.

"As long as you give him some extra money," I told her.

She said, "Of course."

There were two of them, both German women who sat on the rear seat. One had lived in California for eighteen years, then headed back home. Hamburg. They were both extremely nice. We had a good chat on the way to the Bach Dang.

It made me wonder why I had ever disliked Germans.

The Euro travelers we met in Vietnam seemed to be nice people. The Scandinavian, German, French, Dutch, Italian, Finnish, Swiss, British, and others we met along the way. It was Petite who would usually strike up a conversation with them.

No one in Vietnam got the ol' "sock-it-to-you" more than the French got, especially at the Communist museums and landmarks. I admired the French travelers I saw for stoically taking the history lessons on the chin, but I did not think France was as emotionally involved in Vietnam as America was.

As for the Vietnamese, it seemed that young people, whom tourists were most likely to meet as waiters and waitresses, considered all Westerners as being about the same. When I asked about their preferences, most professed not to dislike anyone.

However, an honest friend from Hue filled me in as such:

"We Vietnamese are quite open, and we always try to be very kind to foreigners. In my experience, Japanese are kinder to each other than to foreigners. Vietnamese are kinder to foreigners than to themselves. And Russians aren't kind to anyone."

"TET OFFENSIVE"

In San Diego before we left on the trip, I happened across an issue of *Vietnam*, which had in it an article by Robert Kelley. I liked it so much I took the magazine to Vietnam with me. Our own journey from Da Nang to Hue was the same distance on the same road that 1st Marine field medic Pat White took on the last day of January, 1968.

That was where any resemblance ended.

"The convoy pulled out of Da Nang, and, after experiencing three mechanical breakdowns, arrived in Hue at dusk on January 31. White's company crossed the Perfume River and moved down Le Duan Street to the Citadel. They entered the Citadel through one of the walls and found themselves in the Forbidden Purple City, surrounded by an overgrown maze known as the Imperial Enclosure. Other Marine companies were also positioned inside the Citadel. As his company settled in for the night, White wandered around, admiring the massive walls and gates and the elegant architecture.

The first mortar rounds landed near his company causing chaos and confusion. Many men were killed or wounded, and it seemed those lucky enough to survive were simply meant to be alive. The NVA had his company - and others trying to link up - pinned down. Every attempt by the entrapped companies to move produced a hail of mortar rounds.

He managed to help a few of those who were hit, but he could not respond to every cry. At times, he could only watch as wounded Marines lay dying. The distance to many of the wounded men was not far, only two hundred yards. But every inch was like a mile. The radios were crackling with directions to link up, but with no landmarks to guide them, the young Marines could only guess where to go. It took White's company three days to go that 200 yards.

Twenty eight years later Pat White revisited the Citadel.

'Here I stood,' he told the others with him. 'There were mazes here and here,' he said, gesturing. 'It was hard to link up because we were unfamiliar with this place. At times we were shooting at each other. We entered from a gate in the north wall. There, that's the gate we used. Our company post was set up here.'

He walked toward the gate, now an opening, with the group in tow, stopping halfway. In front of the men stood an old, war-torn stone gazebo. Bullet scars, clearly visible, peppered its exterior. White strode up to it, then walked around it.

'The enemy mortars were set up just outside the wall,' he said, walking toward what had been the enemy positions. He reached the base of the steps that would lead him to the mortar sites and paused for a moment. Then he climbed the steps and stood on the spot where enemy soldiers had lobbed mortar rounds onto his company. 'They had the distance down and could see every move we made,' he said.

We left the mortar positions and reentered the Citadel. Walking past the once-forbidden Purple City, Pat stopped suddenly. His eyes searched the emperor's house and what was left of the wall that had once surrounded it. 'There,' he said, pointing with a trembling finger. 'A friend of mine died there. Would someone take a picture of me?'

He tried to smile but settled for a look of resolve as the shutter clicked.

'It was early in the morning hours, three days after the siege began, that we pulled out of here,' he said. 'There was a Communist flag flying over the Citadel when we silently slipped

131

*through the walls and made our way to the Bach Ho Railway
Bridge, pointing our way to safety.'*

*Now it was time to move on. As we left, Pat gave the Citadel
one final look. His expression seemed to say, 'Goodbye, my friends.
You are gone but not forgotten.'"*

Tet turned out to be the big enchalada, thanks to the
American media circus. From a book review in the same "Tet
Anniversary" issue of **Vietnam**, Col. Harry G. Summers, Jr. wrote:

*"**Big Story** takes a critical look at South Vietnamese
performance in the war. Beginning with a prediction from John
Kenneth Galbraith that the ARVN 'would either disappear into the
woods or join the Viet Cong,' Peter Braestrup notes that
Galbraith's pessimism was due in large measure to the gross
inadequacies of U.S. media coverage by the wire services, TV
networks, newspapers and news magazines.*

*Unreported was the fact that the South Vietnamese did most
of the fighting at Tet, took most of the casualties, and - contrary to
Galbraith's prophesy - did not break under pressure.*

*Another valuable insight is Braestrup's assessment of the
domestic political reaction to the crisis: 'What was striking, and
important, about the public White House posture in February and
March 1968 was how defensive it was. In retrospect, it seemed like
President Johnson was to some degree psychologically defeated by
the threat to Khe Sanh and the onslaught on the cities of Vietnam.'*

*'Rarely has contemporary crisis-journalism turned out, in
retrospect, to have veered so widely from reality,' Braestrup
concludes. 'Essentially, the dominant themes of the words and film
from Vietnam added up to a portrait of defeat for the allies.
Historians, on the contrary, have concluded that the Tet offensive
resulted in a severe military-political setback for Hanoi in the
South. To have portrayed such a setback as a defeat for the other,*

in a major crisis abroad, cannot be counted as a triumph for American journalism.'"

Walter Cronkite first visited the country in mid-1965. He had been briefed on the American strategy of "nation building," as the response to the first use of regular NVA units in the South in 1964. Cronkite had praised this policy, and he believed in it.

General William Westmoreland submitted a "Commander's Estimate of the Situation" in March 1965, defining American strategy in Vietnam.

A. Cause the North to cease its political and military support of the VC.

B. Enable an anti-Communist government to survive so that it ultimately might defeat the VC insurgency.

This was to be implemented in three phases:

1) Employ the American troop buildup to prevent the loss of South Vietnam to the NVA regulars and stop the losing trend by the end of 1965.

2) Employ additional forces during the first half of 1966 to destroy enemy forces in certain high priority areas.

3) By the end of 1967, destroy all enemy use of base areas within South Vietnam.

In the meantime, the nation building efforts would be given time to take effect. (How the military effort would affect nation building was clearly not thought out).

By January 1968 Westmoreland was busy with what he considered to be Phase 3 of a successful operation: Mopping up the enemy bases.

Also in **Vietnam** magazine, General Zeb B. Bradford, aide to General Creighton Abrams at the time of Tet, wrote:

"I was working late in our quarters, a house near Tan San Nhut airport, Saigon's major airfield. It was after 2 a.m., and

Abrams had gone to bed. I heard the sound of nearby gunfire and explosions. I contacted MACV and got the command center. I asked him to send an escort. He told me bluntly that we had to stay out. Enemy elements were between us and the headquarters, and he could not guarantee our safety.

We had to wait. Our line of defense was myself, Sergeant Adams, and a Vietnamese policeman at the front gate. Finally, later in the day, we got out and made it to MACV under heavy escort. But once there, we could not get out. Enemy gunners fired at any aircraft approaching the compound.

MACV headquarters in 1968 was an administrative building, the product of an earlier period when the war consisted of low-intensity counterguerrilla operations conducted in the hinterlands. It was not designed for defense. There were no sandbags, bunkers, revetments or facilities for sustained command operations. Troops from the 101st Airborne Division at nearby Bien Hoa were rushed in to provide security."

Creighton Abrams, at the time the second-most senior American officer in Vietnam, was Westmoreland's chief deputy. Abrams was sleeping in a house in the MACV compound in Saigon, the supreme headquarters, which was as ready for an attack as a boy scout camp would be.

Despite all this, the Tet Offensive was repulsed. All that remained a week later were several NVA and VC units entrenched in a suicidal defense of the Imperial City in Hue. The Communist flag still flew above the citadel's old fortress.

Westmoreland gave the job of removing them to Creighton Abrams.

At this crucial time, Walter Cronkite returned to Vietnam for a second "tour" to report firsthand on the situation after Tet.

Col. Harry G. Summers, Jr., explained what happened:

"It has been argued that the turning point of the war was not so much the 1968 Tet offensive but instead the February 27, 1968, CBS Evening News broadcast featuring Walter Cronkite's assessment of that offensive.

It was reported that President Lyndon Johnson watched the Cronkite broadcast and told his press secretary George Christian that it was 'a turning point, that if he had lost Walter Cronkite he had lost Mr. Average Citizen.' It solidified his decision not to run for president again.

In February 1968 Cronkite traveled to Hue while the battle was still raging and spent an evening at General Abrams' forward headquarters there. Abrams and others sat around a fireplace mulling the deployment of tank forces and separate battalions, speaking of pincer movements, blocking forces, air strikes, and drawing blue arrows on the battle maps.

'It was sickening to me,' Cronkite later recalled. 'They were talking strategy and tactics with no consideration of the bigger job of pacifying and restoring the country. This had come to be total war, not a counterinsurgency. This was a World War II battlefield. The ideas I had talked about in 1965 were gone.'

The United States confused not only itself but also the American people with false notions of counterinsurgency and nation building. When the truth became evident, as it did at Hue during the Tet Offensive, it alienated even those, like Cronkite, who had previously supported our efforts there. It was a self-inflicted wound from which we never recovered."

South of Saigon when Tet was breaking out in the Mekong Delta, Ben Tre became the infamous place where, "It became necessary to destroy the town in order to save it" - a quote that did more for newsman Peter Arnette's career than it did to explain what happened.

The town was destroyed because the VC mortared it and occupied about two-thirds of it. The VC failed to capture the MACV compound in Ben Tre because of a fierce combined American-Vietnamese land and riverine combat defense. As in the rest of South Vietnam, the attack was thwarted, the people who lived there defended themselves, and the Viet Cong were decimated.

Ironically the spirit of Ben Tre was misrepresented to become a catch phrase which fueled opposition to the war.

Lyndon Johnson was particularly devastated by the Tet Offensive because it ruined his plans to get out and disengage. In 1967, he had secretly sent Ellsworth Bunker to Saigon to inform Westmoreland of Johnson's decision to begin pulling out.

Westmoreland agreed, but he thought it would be wiser to put in still a few more troops first, to finish Phase 3 of the battle plan before departing the country in 1969. This would give the South a better chance.

The Tet Offensive ruined these plans.

A month after it happened, the Communists thought they had lost.

The Americans thought they had won, and won they had, but solely a military battle in what was a political war stateside.

In Vietnam itself, the South Vietnamese government did win the political battle of Tet at the time. Southerners generally resented the vicious all-out Communist attack because it occurred on the most sacred day of the year. The successful ARVN defense gave people faith that its government had been tested, and that it could defend them. Last but not least, they witnessed and suffered firsthand from atrocities which took place when Communist cadres moved in on the first night and day.

It was the later ramifications overseas which turned the words "Tet Offensive" into a synonym for defeat.

"APOCALYPSE NOW"

The road snaked up a sheer mountain. About halfway to the top, I could barely make out the white-sand strips of Da Nang behind us. By the time we reached the summit at Hai Van Pass, the view had disappeared into nothingness, lost to the tropical air.

Minh the River was starting to get sentimental on us, and we had been trying to help him with his English a little along the way. At the summit, we pulled over, parked and got out. This was the place "to fish," if you were a vendor, all the bait herded through one narrow pass.

It was a mad scene. Feeding time.

Petite and I ended up with so much crap, it was ridiculous: Post cards, sodas, honey peanuts, Tiger balm, film. But the kids were charming and many of them spoke several languages well. A college-aged man selling postcards spoke fluent American, which he said he had learned at school and had perfected by studying Hollywood movies.

Gun emplacements and pillboxes, most dating from the French days, dotted the mountaintop. It was a good stopover to stretch and have a short "walkabout," although it felt somewhat like an escape when we left.

As we began the descent to Lang Co beach, I realized that an alert Vietnamese twelve-year-old with a couple of years of grade school would learn more English than Minh the River would ever know in this lifetime. It was hopeless at his age.

There was little English he could not mangle.

We pulled over for a drink at a restaurant by the sea at Lang Co. Our table was next to a busload of Japanese tourists, which was entertaining, like a press conference there were so many flashbulbs popping. Some of them took pictures of Petite and me.

So, we may have been going to hell in a bucket but at least we enjoyed the ride, as we took off once again, and made good time amid lush scenery into the royal city of Hue. It had been a pleasant four-hour jaunt.

The bellboy didn't ask permission as he switched on my boom box full-blast and started to reggae up the elevator after we checked into the Century Riverside Hotel. It turned out to be a quite friendly place in a lot of ways. Definitely the snazziest digs we experienced in Vietnam with a nice pool, a massage parlor on the ground floor, and Western prices. Our room balcony had views of the Perfume River and a bridge leading to the Imperial City on the other side.

The afternoon was pure R&R around the pool, writing postcards. Petite talked to a German couple who said Hanoi was cold. Not cool. Cold!

They would know what cold was. Ever the optimist, I assumed it would change before we got there.

There was one slight hang up with Hue, which we discovered the first afternoon. Though the Fahrenheit gauge didn't register much over 95, it *felt* at least 140. There was so much standing water in the area - rivers, moats, lakes, almost a wetland - that I'd been in sauna baths that felt crisper.

But sitting by the pool, it wasn't a real problem.

After finishing off the post cards, I consulted the **Rough Guide**. Where to go for dinner?

"Hue's two most famous restaurants, run by a family of deaf-mutes, stand next door to each other just outside the Citadel walls. There's little to choose between them: both have lots of atmosphere, good prices and the food's fine, catering to the tourist trade with Hue specialties, noodle soups, and banana pancakes."

138

After dark, Minh dropped us off in front of the twin eateries. He drove off to find a parking place. We were told to walk up a set of stairs that overlooked the kitchen.

I formerly owned a restaurant. I've seen a few kitchens in my day. Glancing down from the stairwell, this one did not look promising with non-refrigerated meat and produce laying about like it was a Calcutta market. Not to mention the flies.

When we got to the top floor, the first thing I noticed was scribbling on the wall by customers in various languages, all praising the fare. The message next to my chair on the crowded balcony said, in Italian, "This place has good food."

A cute, sassy waitress appeared.

I glanced at the menu and ordered a Tuborg beer.

She informed me that they were out of Tuborg. "We have Huda. It's the same thing and it's cheaper."

"Sign me up," I said, and ordered one for Minh as well.

When the waitress returned, I read the beer label. It said that Huda was brewed in Hue with "Danish Technology."

The young waitress grabbed a device sitting on top of an adjacent table. She held my beer bottle and violently slammed the top with this strange-looking thing, sending the beer cap shooting over the balcony like a little Saber jet, where it crashed to the pavement below.

Impressive Vietnamese Beer-Opener Technology.

She left us alone to read the menus. Petite and Minh started chatting in Vietnamese.

My eyes wandered to the street below. A Citadel wall was directly across the busy street. A group of cyclo drivers had gathered under a lamp. While foreigners were relatively prevalent in this area, 95 percent of the people walking and riding by were Vietnamese.

A flustered teenager bounded up the stairwell and threw her school satchel on a table next to us. I had wanted to have a further chat with the first waitress, but this girl grabbed a note pad and ran up to us, still panting from the jog up.

Unlike the first girl, this one was a deaf mute. She took our food orders and did a perfect job, getting everything correctly by reading our lips.

Even at night outside on the balcony, it was sweltry.

The beer was excellent, Minh agreed. We both ordered another liter from the third person to appear, a middle-aged man who was also deaf-mute.

I was hardly surprised when a fourth waiter brought up our food. I dug into the piping hot dish named "Barbecue Beef," which tasted exactly like "Pork Skewer" back at my favorite Vietnamese restaurant in San Diego.

The name of the place in San Diego was *A Dong*. Literally, it meant "Asia East."

Every Vietnamese restaurant, in which I've eaten, from London to San Francisco to Hong Kong, to Vietnam itself, has lacked in comparison. So to say that the barbecue beef compared with a dish at *A Dong* was great praise, indeed.

When the "Spring Rolls" arrived, I decided they were even better than those at my favorite spot were.

Except for the garlic *Rau Muong* on the river at Phan Thiet, this was the only instance during our trip where the food in Vietnam was as good or better than it was at home. It had mostly to do with raw materials. Restaurants in Vietnam had to be incredibly inexpensive to compete, and the government owned most. But cheap prices were incompatible with quality meat and poultry. Seafood was the best bet, really, but due to a genetic defect, I could not abide that.

Petite ordered a plate of *Rau Muong* at *Lac Thiet*. However, it was never as good again as the first time because they failed to clip the leaves and it came out more like collard greens than baby asparagus.

When we departed Petite and I stood on the street waiting for Minh to get the van. The waiters and waitresses we had met came out to say good-bye and come back tomorrow. That sort of behavior made us feel special, although it buttressed my own delusions of grandeur. Almost everyone in Vietnam treated Petite like visiting royalty, which she happened to be, but it didn't go to *her* head.

Minh dropped us off at the *Apocalypse Now* bar. He asked if he could leave and if we could walk home. After two liters of beer, he was finished with driving, and perhaps somewhat embarrassed that I paid for everything when he was with us.

It was only five blocks back to the hotel. Petite and I agreed that we could handle the hike.

We visited three separate *Apocalypse Now* bars in Vietnam: in Saigon, Hue, and Hanoi.

I enjoyed the one in Hue best. All were owned by the same young Vietnamese fellow, and all three sold tee shirts. That was the prize. They had fine logos, possibly copied from the movie poster. Best of all they had Large, XL, and XXL sizes made of good material. Prices ranged from $5 to $8, triple the average price but triple the quality. And they fit the gringo body, as opposed to most of the merchandise available in Vietnam.

Perhaps I had expected too much, but the establishment in Saigon was a disappointment, like any run-of-the-mill beach bar in San Diego or across the border in Mexico. The music in the bar in Saigon was lousy, yet it was the only one with girls sitting around. It did not occur to me to buy a shirt there until I saw Liam's while we sat by the pool at the Rex.

The bar in Hue was a step up from the one in Saigon, and was decorated mostly with white-painted English graffiti on its black walls. ***CHARLEY DON'T SURF*** one of them announced.

With the horror of that concept slowly sinking in, I ordered a Huda.

Petite did not like being in the hot, humid room. She was allergic to alcohol. And allergic to me when I drank too much of it.

I asked the bartender if I could see the tee shirt collection.

Of the designs which each of the three bars had on its shirts, the ones from the bar in Hue were the finest: An image of the Citadel on the back. These tee shirt forays were pretty much the extent of my shopping in the country.

I bought five of them and ordered another beer.

Petite became what I call: "bitchy."

We had a short spat, while the bartenders looked on. After that, we stopped talking to each other altogether.

I checked the place out.

Damn good music, Allman Brothers. Too bad the bar wasn't air-conditioned. On a far wall were surrealistic art forms; rounded shapes suggesting choppers and whirly blades - the penultimate symbol of the war. A mural of decrepit Marlon Brando, Cambodian get up and all, dominating a wall by the dance floor.

Ah... the horror.

Apocalypse Now, the movie, was one of my favorites. In retrospect, it had a heavy hand in shaping what I thought I knew about the war in Vietnam in the 1970s.

But the first time I saw it, a few scenes seemed to stretch credibility. Not the parts toward the end with Marlon B. upriver, either.

The most cartoon-like aspects of the film to me were scenes where halfway upriver, Martin Sheen had to grab and pull a sergeant across the table to get gasoline for the boat. And especially a night scene at the last GI outpost by Cambodia, where a bridge had collapsed into the water. Aimless continual fighting. Flares popping. Tracer fire. No one in charge along the frontier.

Scarcely a year after the movie came out, I came to know an older man in his mid-forties. He had the desk across from mine at work, and he was a nice fellow who had once played in the navy band.

He told me that he had recurring problems. Flashbacks to when he sawed-into-two a soldier on the riverbank with his boat's twin .50-caliber machineguns, known as "The Bad Boys." He had served in the "brown-water navy" on a river similar to the one in the movie.

Now, ten years later, at his desk he was taking a break from adjusting fixed assets for the finance department. We started talking about the movie.

I told him how much I liked it. Although the scene upriver where no one was in charge had been a bit cartoon-like, didn't he think?

The man froze, visibly shivering in his corporate cubicle.

I asked, "What's wrong?"

"That scene gave me nightmares every damned night for three months," he said.

"NAKED CITY"

Air-conditioning bit at our toes in the room at the Century Riverside. Before sunrise I awoke to discover I had a case of the trots, my first of the trip.

Nevertheless, down in the hotel dining room they were serving the tastiest fried eggs ever, Vietnamese eggs, as well as fresh bread, butter, and banana pancakes washed down with coffee.

By 8:00 a.m. Petite and I were outdoors. The temperature was almost pleasant. Minh the River pulled up on time.

We took the van over the first bridge of three lined up across the Perfume River. We then drove around, apparently aimlessly, for thirty minutes as our intrepid driver tried in vain to locate the entrance to the Purple City, which was also called the Forbidden City, or the royal quarters.

First, we drove over a moat and through the southeastern gate into the Citadel, which covered an area of several square miles. Shops, houses, and streets crisscrossed under shade trees within the compound. Across from a fortress by the river Minh found the entrance to the Purple City. This enclosure comprised only a small portion of the total area behind the Citadel walls.

Minh dropped us off at a plaza, and we asked him to return in three hours.

Petite and I had known each other almost twenty years. We had been married for three-fourths of that time. It was an hour into our walk through the imperial grounds and we were resting in the shade of the Royal Reading Pavilion, a building apart from the others, when Petite made me realize how little we sometimes know one another.

Puffing a menthol cigarette, she said, "I grew up in a villa behind the Citadel wall. We had to move when I was six. I used to come over here and play, but the royal city was awful then. No maintenance, the canals filled with sludge. Not many people here. It was a lonely place. It's good that tourists have started coming to Vietnam. Now they pay to see it, and the people here can afford to keep it nice."

"You grew up *here*?" I asked.

I was desperate to find the villa, before I remembered that 90% of everything behind the Citadel's walls had been razed at one time or another since then.

The private villa was hard to square with the parents' graveyard in that musky field on the outskirts of Saigon. What a precipitous drop from privileged life behind the walls of the Citadel in Hue.

The family had a lot of money when they lived in Hue, but it was based on landholdings in Quang Ngai Province.

Father sent his eldest son, the future Famous Artist, to there from Hue in order to live with his own mother, the boy's paternal grandmother, because the son was lazy even at that age. Father figured his mother would shape up the kid.

Meanwhile, the Viet Minh came into Quang Ngai and took over the province. The Famous Artist and Grandmother lived on a bowl of rice a day, which the Communists gave them. The family's extensive land holdings were all in the one province, so during this time there was no income from the property.

Father started to travel to Cambodia and Laos; bringing back cattle and hogs, on the hoof.

"Soon," Petite said, "our villa in the Citadel looked like a ranch in Texas." She remembered that it was fun as a child to have all the animals around.

After seven years, at age sixteen the Famous Artist escaped

from the communist-held province. Mother hated the paternal grandmother for letting eldest son come there, then not protect him or get him out safely before the Communists took over.

The family reunited in Hue. The Famous Artist hated his father, as a consequence, and remained forever bitter over what had happened.

Father moved the family to Saigon and went into the construction business. After the Viet Minh moved out of Quang Ngai in 1954, he sold much of the family land, little by little, mostly to the local farmers. Father then lost all of the money in his construction ventures. By the end of his life at age 49, the family sometimes could afford rice and nothing else to eat. They did, however, manage to send Petite to Catholic school to provide a good education for her.

Household servants, not her mother, raised Petite. After Father's death, Mother ceded all her considerable power within the family to the Famous Artist, her favorite child. He became a bully, of sorts.

Petite said, "I tried to stay away from him as much as possible."

I sighed. "There's a million stories in the naked city, right?"

Petite agreed.

We strolled to the edge of the inner walls, by a small meadow with a raised foundation on the ground that once held the King's palace. Nearby, I noticed a gazebo-shaped structure next to an entrance through the wall. It had a number of bullet holes blasted into it, bigger than AK-47 rounds. I sat down on the grass beside the gazebo. The door to the gate through the inner wall was open. It was straight through this opening where VC mortars were placed during the battle of Tet when medic Pat White arrived on that fateful evening.

We began the hike back to the entrance.

Most of the area was a field with a few standing walls. Streams and ponds laced the green, and it felt like a wet sauna.

Halfway back, I received urgent orders from the cobwebs at Command and Control: Find a Rest Room!

Control was flagging. I had 30 seconds before **"Bombs Away."**

I took off running, which didn't help matters.

At the public bathrooms, there was an excruciating wait to buy toilet paper. I fidgeted behind a wench who seemed to be purchasing enough for her entire neighborhood. (Yes, I said *buy* toilet paper).

After it was said and done, this important tale had a Hollywood ending. That's right. Everything came out okay.

Hue was the only place in the world I've been where it occurred to me that I might actually be in the process of being cooked. A slow but steady steam of the precious body fluids in God's little wok by the Perfume River. Simply hike around town for a week and you'll be "sunny side up." Two weeks for hard-boiled. Go figure why the Nguyens moved the royal family there, when they could have chosen Nha Trang.

The weather alone would drive most of us crazy.

The King had something like 150 females at his disposal. He would choose one every night in an official ceremony. I read about a certain eighty-year-old monarch who had to be carried into the royal bedroom because he was unable to walk. Then of course it took forever to get things going with the fifteen-year-old country girl, who was probably terrified.

Not exactly a Cinderella tale.

As for the kings, nowadays in California they've made people like that register with the police as soon as they move into town.

"RED LIGHT"

I had originally planned to write a little something about massage parlors.

Then I figured: *Naw!*

But rethinking the subject later, it seemed almost dishonest not to say something about sex in the Orient. It wasn't just Vietnam. Many of the male tourists and "business" travelers in Asia as a whole were there primarily for sex. That was, you didn't see them on the sightseeing bus. They were in the bars, back in the hotel room, or around the pool.

Sex was no simple cottage industry in most of Southeast Asia, but it was less obvious in Vietnam than in most of the other countries in the area. Nothing compared to Thailand; and the Philippines was second only to Thailand.

The kid we rented the hut from on the beach at Nha Trang wore a tee shirt that read: "No Child Sex." There was an instance when we were at the Sailing Club there, where a German man in his fifties sat alone with a young boy, who was ostensibly practicing his English.

Who knows?

In the Philippines, kids who sell themselves to men were known as "billy boys." There were probably a few of those everywhere. Actually, it didn't get much worse anywhere than Balboa Park in San Diego after dark.

As for night clubs, Liam and I originally planned to sneak over to The Bumble Bee, its sign flashing right across from the Rex in Saigon, but we never got around to it. By the way, the girl at the Rex swimming pool who made such a big impression on us turned out to be a Japanese tourist there with her boyfriend, who was whom she was looking for. Not us.

I did have six massages in Vietnam, including two each at the Rex and the Century Riverside. Generally, you got what you paid for. The Rex cost about fifteen bucks and was the most expensive. It was the best. It was better than my usual $60 rub at the Las Vegas Hilton, and the guy at the Hilton wrote a book on massage technique.

The trick was to find a place that had rails suspended in the rooms. What made the Rex massages so good was that the girls would stand on your back, hold onto the rails for balance, and use their entire weight to dig their toes into your muscles.

Thai Massage.

The Rex girls came from a government school, which provided training. They weren't weighed down by excess clothing, either. However, I was never propositioned at the Rex.

I've already described the tortuous beating I took on the beach at Nha Trang. That was the cheapest massage I got in Vietnam. Then there was one in Da Nang from a big old gal, who charged $7. Petite walked back from shopping into our room toward the end. She told Petite, "I got him good!"

Petite cackled.

You could imagine what that one was like.

At the Century Riverside in Hue, it was $8 for a massage.

After dark, a bevy of young beauties lined up in front of the massage area by the pool. Form fitting short shorts, nasty footwear. Friendly, too. I should have known.

My first clue was three minutes into the massage, I heard a passionate "**AHHH-HEEEEEE-YAH**" from an adjoining room.

Next, a man's voice; a light spatter of Korean, or Chinese, or something.

When my time eventually came, I turned down the

proposition, of course. For the record, she asked for 300,000 Dong. And that was for what Bill Clinton would not even consider "sexual relations," although the patron in the adjoining room might not have agreed with him.

The price sounded expensive, which was one thing changed since the war.

During the war Vietnam was, in certain places, the Wild Wild West. A stewardess friend of mine working for World Airlines told me about a bar she went to in Saigon in 1971. It was open air on a second story, crowded with GIs draped over the chairs at midday. The only item on the menu was Coca Cola for a dollar each. With it, came a packet of powder that was mixed in the cola.

Heroin and Coke.

When we were in Da Nang in the van, going from the beach to the Cham Museum, my questioning turned Minh the River visibly nervous the only time on the trip.

Cagily, I commented, "I hear a lot of the young people in Vietnam like to smoke marijuana."

Minh the River played dumb.

Petite said, "He doesn't know what 'marijuana' is."

"Joints. Smoke. Reefer. Weed. Boo... Hashish?"

Minh said it was *Very* expensive.

"How much?"

"*You Go Jail!*" he said.

"No, no, no," I laughed. "Not for me!"

I asked Petite to explain to him in Vietnamese that I was simply curious. By this time, he knew I was a writer. It was for the book.

But Petite didn't tell him anything.

She said, "He *knows* that."

Didn't sound like it to me. I asked, "Do the Euro kids you cart around ever get high in the van along the way?"

He said that they usually asked him to buy it for them but he never did. Minh also volunteered that, yes, most of the people who smoked marijuana in Vietnam were the young, and it was somewhat prevalent in high school.

"A disgusting breakdown in the moral fabric of society," I noted. "How much would it cost for a girl?"

This did not seem to make him uptight as the narco grilling had done. Like: How much was a jar of pickles? Or the current cost of lettuce?

"Hundred dollars pretty girl." Minh added, "That what cost white man."

I said, "But I've got a tan."

He started laughing.

Petite had had it.

My translator quit on me.

"WHEN WE LEAVE"

Visiting the Purple City on Friday, we found a few buildings still standing. A lot of it was like a Roman meadow. The first building we encountered through the gate was Thai Hoa Palace, the Emperor's official greeting area. It was not a palace but a large room. Photos were not allowed in order to preserve the original lacquer paint on the wooden columns, done in the color of dry blood, truly royal red.

Thai Hoa and the Reading Pavilion were the only buildings not severely damaged during the trials and tribulations of the past two centuries.

We nearly walked out of the Purple City without visiting what turned out to be my favorite part of it.

Petite pointed up toward the top of the outer wall. People milling around. Up the steps, we found a huge polished brass bell. This was a pavilion where the Emperor reviewed his troops. A platform on high, a parade ground below on the stone plaza. The four-sided view was fantastic.

A humongous red flag with a yellow star fluttered above the black fortress by the Perfume. The wide, hazel river drifted out into a mist.

To either side: moats, ramparts, expansive green lawns.

The rear view was the Purple City we had just toured.

Yellow ceramic tile railing decorated the reviewing stand. The tile on the trim looked like bamboo. Elegant.

The next morning, Saturday, we hopped aboard a boat and went up the Perfume River nine miles, then back, stopping at two spots along the way. About three hours round trip. We invited Minh along for his first boat ride.

A family lived aboard. Inside, the boat was painted shiny blue with artwork, family photos, furniture, and a calendar. The vessel housed a baby girl, a small boy, Mom and Dad. I asked if I could take a photo of the baby sleeping peacefully in her bassinet. The mother nervously said no, and Petite quickly explained that it was a "No-No" to take pictures of people sleeping because they looked too much like they were dead. The inference was that mere appearance could somehow manifest itself in reality.

On the river were many boat people, as well as little butts hanging over the side. The water in the river didn't look foul or smell bad, and there was less trash than in San Diego Bay, but when Petite asked if I wanted to jump overboard for a swim, I declined based on the fanny factor.

On the cruise up, we stopped at Thien Mu pagoda and Hon Chen temple. Neither was remarkable, but there were numerous Asian pastoral scenes along the banks of the river. On the way back, I took a picture of the railway bridge that the Marines marched over after the battle of Tet; the ugliest bridge of the several spanning the river, it still had wire strung around each base, but it had a place in the American experience. Next to it the huge black citadel seemed like a low-slung armored tank with no turret, rising from behind the riverbank; an almost impregnable stone fortress where the Communists held out in 1968 flying a smaller version of the banner that now fluttered lazily.

Before disembarkation at tour's end on a dock next to our hotel, we stopped in the back cabin and saw the three-month-old baby swinging in a wicker bassinet. She was finally awake. Tiny monkey skulls with oversized hollow eye sockets were attached to the crib.

Jumping onto the dock, I asked Petite what the monkeys

were all about, not that I couldn't have guessed. As I thought:

"To chase away the devil," she said.

Poor little thing had broken into sudden tears in her bassinet seeing me coming down the narrow walkway in the boat. Rocking it auspiciously with cornpone Yankee weight, firing off a snapshot.

An omen for the afternoon, no doubt:

Our visit to Thuan An Beach.

Without getting into the gory details, this was what I wrote in my diary:

"Minh the River wanted to take us to the beach after his first river ride because he knew I liked beaches. Sweet, gentle guy - we're lucky he's our driver - but:

THUAN BEACH SUCKS!@!

* Vendors won't leave you alone.

* Water is dark brown close to shore! Dangerous rip, I could hardly stand up. Jellyfish floating past on the treacherous tide. Corpus Delecti-Port Aransas squared.

* Got ripped off for 40,000 for beach shelter. Then 20,000 a Huda!

* Minh even got hit up for 2,000 to park. That's after we paid 20,000 to get in.

Everyone in the van was pissed off on the way back to Hue."

There was a lot of Ugly American II revisited in that entry. But in this case, we hadn't asked what it cost *before* we bought it.

And each of us knew "The Golden Rule." So we were madder at ourselves, I think, than at them.

The best part of this story occurred after we returned to San Diego. A photo I had taken that day.

Two beer can soldiers, recently killed in action, guarded the top of a white plastic ice chest.

I glanced up from a book.

By the hand, a child led a grizzled old blind woman toward our blue canvass beach shelter. The pensioner wore a colorful blue-purple blouse that caught my eye.

I put the book to my face and started reading again, until I heard Petite explode in laughter, "She's supposed to be blind!"

Petite had a slim 120-mil cigarette in hand. She said, "Her eyes leaped when she saw me take out my cigarettes."

The old woman now had a hand out, speaking Vietnamese.

"She's asking for one."

My wife handed the grinning beach woman one of the most protracted cigarettes manufactured on earth. Next, Petite reached into her purse to pull out some money.

I grabbed the camera and zoomed in on the woman's lined face from six feet away.

Conehat. Bamboo Pole. Colorful purple blouse.

The sun had done to hers what it did to skin: Spot it brown.

Squeezing the lengthy cancerstick with bony digits and cupping her hands lighting it against the breeze, she pulled in a cloud of smoke like Charley Chan. Two sun-baked fingers balanced the nicotine delivery instrument.

I named the photo: "Surgeon General of Vietnam."

On arrival at Thuan An beach, we had stood at the gate, as Petite tried to negotiate the entrance fee by telling fables such as: "They told us it was only 15,000 at the hotel."

They weren't buying that one today.

A girl selling pineapples came up and started to talk to me in almost perfect Californeese: American English.

Young Conehat.

It didn't jive with my preconceptions.

I looked at the pineapples on the swing pole she toted. None were sliced. I pictured myself dragging one around the rest of the day. Actually I didn't want one at all, I decided, even though I loved pineapple.

I told her, "Sure, when we leave I'll buy one."

It was not a conscious lie at the time. Vietnam had a certain charm. The people might have bugged me at times with their begging and such, yet in the South they were generally so likeable that it made me, as a foreigner, also want to please them in return.

The pineapple girl showed up later with all of her buddies. They were in high school, and worked at the beach in the afternoons to pay the tuition. My friend who had spoken English so well pulled out a music tape out and handed it to me: "The Eagles Greatest Hits."

She explained that she studied the tape to perfect her accent.

"*There's a dark desert highway. Cool wind in her hair... The smell of olitas...* what's that?" she asked.

"That's *fajitas*, kiddo. Espanol. The smell of fat on an open fire."

We sang together, "*Welcome to the Hotel California.*"

We laughed. I advised her, "Take the graduate course and get a Beach Boys tape... 409. All over La Jolla. Waimea Bay. Come on the Sloop John B, the whole nine yards."

She asked, "Buy a pineapple?"

Her price was only four times higher than it should have been. However, to the best of my recollection I fully intended to purchase one.

"Sure, when we leave," I said.

I soon got involved in fighting the wild surf; trying to stand in the violent current, dodging jellyfish tentacles sweeping past, hoping if it happened I could take the beast head-on. Better chance to spin away without getting stung At least that was the game plan.

I made it to shore somehow. Then it was 90 degrees in the shade on the beach again. The cooler water rejuvenated me but it was only a battle, not the war unfortunately. We lost that one arguing with the beach-hut fellow over his absurd pricing policy.

"I'll never trust another Vietnamese again," I proclaimed, storming for the exit, and refusing to buy a pineapple from another of the beach girls Petite had now designated.

The tantrum embarrassed my wife in front of her native countrymen. She was behind me, shaking her head over the childish display.

I hoped we would see my fellow *Eagles* fan in the parking lot, where she was when we came in. But she wasn't there.

Next it was Minh's turn. Some local yokel came up to collect a fee out in the parking lot. There was a heated exchange before Minh coughed up the money.

As for the pineapple girl, I put it in my diary as such:
"She came back several times. I said 'When we leave.'
But she wasn't around when we left.
I felt bad about it - Nguoi My (American Person) angst."

On the road to Hue, we were deciding where to eat dinner. Petite and Minh told me about the most famous restaurant in Hue, *Ong Tao*, and another one. They asked me to pick.

"Let's go the famous one," I said.

We got back to the hotel. Petite wanted to go see an ancestor's mausoleum, which had many bronze soldiers guarding it.

I wanted to go to the pool, maybe try a massage.

Petite and Minh took off.

In the hotel room, I opened the guide. No *Ong Tao*

restaurant was even listed.

Roughly translated, *"Ong Tao"* meant "hibachi," or "cooking broiler." It had a double meaning, as well, referring to an annual ceremony performed in Vietnamese homes one week before Tet. The first ceremony was held in the kitchen to say farewell to Ong Tao, now a spirit, on the journey to God. Ong Tao then reported directly to God on the family's current affairs. This was so God would know what was happening in case He wanted to help out with solving their problems. On the third day of Tet, the second ceremony took place, welcoming back the kitchen spirit.

Saturday evening when we arrived, an empty tour bus was parked in the dirt alley next door to *Ong Tao* restaurant. I hopped out of the van. My left knee sent bolts shivering up the leg nerves; the result of an afternoon massage, the last one I had in Vietnam.

I hobbled through the doorway after Petite and Minh. God, the place was noisy. White walls. Tile floor.

The man who met us at the door escorted us to a table in front of the manager's desk. An office had been set up in one corner of the dining floor. A beer sign told us that this was a privately owned business.

The folks making the racquet were seated together at long tables which took up two-thirds of the dining room. Now and then, hysterical screams of laughter would come pealing across.

I guessed they were peasants, and off the last turnip truck. Hard. Not a good-looking person among the fifty seated in the area.

Unusual for Vietnam, I thought.

I looked at the menu.

They were easy to find on this one, almost leaping off the page:

Sucking Pig (Order In Advance)
All Kinks of Colas

The Vietnamese-language menus that were handed to Petite and Minh had three times the pages mine did.

Our waiter dropped by. Minh and I ordered Hudas. Petite, a cola.

Away from the noisy group of strangers, a beautiful girl was staring at our table. She started into "exercises," hands over her head.

I gazed back at her.

She was with two Korean guys fitted out in brand-name sleeveless shirts and jogging pants. They ignored her. She wore a white dress to mid-knee, with interesting red high-heels.

Minh now looked up from his menu and caught me staring back at her. He informed me that she was from Saigon. He knew her. A working girl.

Indeed.

The waiter brought our drinks and took the food order. I decided to try the specialty of Hue, which also happened to be my favorite dish at *A Dong*: Charbroiled Grape Leaves.

Hamburger with spices, wrapped in grape leaves.

The waiter scurried away with our order.

I had the open menu in front of me. I looked *again*.

No Bleeping Prices!

After the beach experience and all.

Petite said only, "Don't worry."

"Well, fine," I said, perturbed about getting ripped off twice in one day, until shouting from over by the long tables caught my attention. It looked as if some sort of gang fight between older men was about to break out. The women had left to get back on the turnip bus. The dispute was about the charges on the bill. One of the customers waved it in the air, as if flying a kite. Then he spat on it - a unique protest, which heretofore I had not witnessed despite ten years in the restaurant business.

The manager, who had been sitting at his desk counting money moments before, suddenly appeared across the room.

I asked Minh where the bus people were from.

"Ha Noi," he said.

Hanoi? Jesus.

The restaurant manager took the offensive and got in the spitter's face, yelling back at him. Soon they were moving toward us, shouting at one another. One of the calmer men from Hanoi started to hold back his pugnacious buddy.

I could see that the feisty one was drunk.

Sneaking a peek to the opposite side of the room, I noticed the two Korean guys by themselves chatting away. No Miss Saigon.

The room quieted after the drunk spat toward the waiter as a parting gesture. I supposed they had anted up the entire charge because the manager, again safely behind his desk, wore a satisfied grin.

The restaurant started filling once more with Vietnamese. Then a group of twelve Americans, men and women and two college kids, came in and sat at the table nearest us.

The Americans seemed to be talking louder than people normally did. I could pick out almost every word they said.

"... a choice of sleeping with three women - Lorena Bobbit, Tonya Harding, or Hillary Clinton - and which one would he choose?"

Minh the River started into an emotional going-away speech to Petite and I.

Eyes watering, he told us that the past week had felt like a vacation for him, as well.

Once again, I told Minh how lucky we were to have him as our driver in Vietnam. I proposed a toast.

The food came. As we ate, Minh the River filled us in on what to expect tomorrow in Hanoi. He warned us it would be dangerous. Don't go out after dark. Pickpockets even in daytime.

The folks were so poor, if you cooked a chicken in the North, you had to shut the doors tight so the smell couldn't escape. If the neighbors smelled that fat chicken, they would reasonably assume you were rich all of a sudden, and report you to the police thinking you had stolen something.

I looked to Petite for help on this one.

She had never been to Hanoi, either.

Between mouthfuls, Minh explained how the Northerners often carved wooden fish to pour fish sauce upon in the privacy of their homes, pretending they had fresh fish to eat with their rice.

I was speechless for a change.

He added, "Just recent get *erectrisitree.*"

Electricity. And plumbing too.

Petite confirmed that she had heard the same thing about electric power in the North. "Maybe we should head home a week early," she said.

Did the North suck, or what?

I said to Petite, "We wanted to see Ha Long Bay. Didn't we, honey?"

She thought for a second and nodded. "We can take anything for a week."

We were to fly out in the morning. An hour and a half, as opposed to a rough two-day drive. We had heard the roads were awful in the North.

The bill arrived.

Petite pulled out some cash and treated us to dinner. She showed me the tally, a bargain, but agreed that Vietnamese food was better in San Diego. The grape leaves in Hue were tiny.

On the way out of *Ong Tao* restaurant, I stopped at the

nearby table, leaned over to the big fellow in the head chair, and said in a theatrical whisper: *"Lorena Bobbit."*

All at the American table laughed.

We were almost out the door when the big guy shouted at me, **"Hey, you weren't supposed to hear that!"**

Hey, *really?*

"THOOP!"

They were not close calls. But they were the closest I got to Vietnam during the war, and they were all in 1966.

The first was a letter at mail call in basic training in February. Mom forwarded it to me at Fort Leonard Wood with a funny note because it was my draft induction notice.

"Fooled them, eh?"

If I had been drafted and had begun ten weeks of basic training in March, plus another eight weeks of advanced infantry training school, I would have arrived in Vietnam in September, 1966.

In April, my German language Army Security Agency class met for the first time at Ft. Meade Maryland to begin training. By this time, almost four more years of army life now looked a lot different than it had in civvies signing on the dotted line. I became friends with an eighteen-year-old from Massachusetts, who came up with the brilliant idea of us both signing up for officer's school.

O.C.S.

I did give it some thought, a scary idea looking back.

After a couple of days I decided not to bother. It would have gotten me out of the army only six months earlier. And rumors had it that Second Looies had the highest KIA rate.

The training class at Ft. Meade was run by civilians and it turned out to be great fun living on the East Coast. It was like any other school I had been to, except we were in the army. NSA Headquarters was the big building in the neighborhood, instead of the Texas Tower.

As an aside, after being deep in the bowels of NSA

Headquarters, I should say that if all the stuff on the **X-Files** were really happening, NSA would surely not be the one in charge.

They couldn't possibly pull off anything that clever.

At Ft. Meade through September, I dated the base commander's daughter. She felt comfortable at the officer's club, where her friends were. One of them was a Second Looey in Eleventh Armored Cav., who was running armored tanks around in preparation for Vietnam. He told me that he had signed up for jungle training school during the two-week leave that was granted before assignment overseas.

I was astounded. Not everyone would head directly home and start partying until he was tossed on the troop train?

This guy was impressive, leaving nothing to chance because everyone knew that the snake-eater school down in Florida wasn't a day at the beach. It was day with the bitch.

Fourteen straight.

I shipped out to Germany in September, 1966. A couple of months later, I got a letter from the base commander's daughter.

In our lieutenant friend's first month in Vietnam, both his legs were blown off by a land mine. And he was alive.

"It began on a Sunday in September 1966. On this day the Vietnamese in their pagodas tried to appease all the souls of the unburied dead. Wandering souls. Those of beggars, prostitutes, and soldiers."

These were opening lines of a documentary filmed in Vietnam by Pierre Schoendoerfer who had been a French soldier at Dien Bien Phu, having returned thirteen years later. His film, *The Anderson Platoon*, won an Academy Award in 1967.

I came across it by chance at Blockbuster.

It did for me what no film had done since *Fixed Bayonet* in the early 1950s. It completely deglorified war. (Later in the editing phase of this book, I would say that Mallick's *The Thin Red Line* and *Saving Private Ryan* were as good as it got in this area, but the movies had yet to appear when this chapter was written).

The Anderson Platoon was filmed during the rainy season in September and October. The French-accented English narration was hard to follow. The producer must have saved money on film, the black-and-white was so grainy. But this hour-long documentary depicted the essence and reality of combat as it followed a U.S. army platoon for six weeks, much of it in the bush. In 1966 there was none of the drugs and disobeying officers and such in the field. The troops in the film seemed almost cherry. No peace signs. No dope. No harming civilians. No burning huts. No stealing.

Many of them seemed to worship the prostitutes they met.

It was not a propaganda piece for either side, but an honest depiction during which the producer claimed to have learned more about America than he did about Vietnam. But Schoendoerfer already knew about war in Vietnam. For the uninitiated, the film was about the reality of combat. A depressing but worthy account.

It showed that the war was indeed a lower class affair, and that not all the poor people in America were minorities. Personally, I had forgotten that fact, living in Southern California. Pierre Schoendoerfer seemed particularly infatuated with two of the soldiers in the platoon. The first, a "Blues Singer from Alabama." A black GI who could sing well and often did, strumming his guitar in camp. The blues seemed more appropriate to the actual situation than any Creedence Clearwater song ever did.

The director's second favorite was a white boy named Reece from South Carolina; the Gomer-Pyle type.

I saw a lot of those in the Army.

The cameras followed Reece into Saigon for a 7-day pass. The place was almost unrecognizable to me. American or Vietnamese MPs were stationed on most downtown street corners.

165

More garbage was along the sidewalks than now. Soldiers and military vehicles were conspicuous. The autos were French.

"Upon arriving in Saigon, he wanted to rent a room with a private bathroom. He had never had one before. Then he wanted to go see the elephants at the zoo."

Reece never got around to the elephants. He started out bar hopping downtown. The next scene showed him the following morning buying a guitar and some underwear for a girl with a beehive hairdo.

Later, he and the girl stood outside a roll of barbed wire along one of Saigon's boulevards to watch a military parade commemorating the anniversary of the independence of South Vietnam. Prime Minister Ky came by, waving at the crowd, standing in an open Cadillac convertible. Afterward, there was the sound of an explosion. People running in the street. Shots going off. The VC had started firing at the reviewing stand for the parade. It was chaotic.

"Reece says he feels safer in his platoon than here."

He blew his money in the big city after four days and returned broke to his platoon before his leave was officially over.

The so-called "Anderson platoon" was part of the 1st Infantry Division, and was stationed to the south of Quang Ngai in both Binh Dinh province on the coast and westward into the Central Highlands. U.S. troops aided local villagers with medicine and helicopter evacuation to civilian hospitals, though they often discovered military equipment hidden in baskets of vegetables, and even received fire from some of these same villages.

Without saying so, the film made it plain that the Americans went wherever they wanted to in Vietnam. And quickly.

The platoon loaded onto choppers at 7 a.m. one morning in October 1966 after Reece had returned. They took off for LZ Gigi, the crest of a nearby hill. But in the air, they got word that two

Chinooks had been shot down at a village ten miles away, so B Company and the platoon were diverted south to the battle. A "VC" battalion was encircled, according to the radio.

The platoon landed, as other gunships raked the opposite field with rockets and machine gun fire, and the radio told them that a VC company was trying to escape across a stream.

The platoon headed along the stream, policing up dead bodies and many weapons along the way. They pulled two wounded Vietnamese out of tunnels, one with a nasty shoulder wound, and happened upon an abandoned enemy camp in the jungle. Although I would have been wary of booby traps, they didn't seem particularly worried.

Next they came upon an enemy soldier in another tunnel. He came up, hands in the air.

"Ask him if they's any mo' o' his comrades, any more VC that want to give up."

"He says he's from the North."

"Sgt. Athern, come take charge of this prisoner here."

Sgt. Athern was now on the radio, calling the gunships above:

"Over One Six. We got one prisoner of war. Pistol belt, canteen, black pajamas, no haircut, no weapon. You want me to move him? I've got Lima Zulu right here. Or I can wait for a signed Oh-Two, or I can hold him till he's picked up. Over."

It sounded much like something we have grown used to on the "Cops" television show.

Tit! Tit! Tit!

Sudden AK-47 fire.

Tot! Tot! The unit returned fire with M-16s, everyone now down in prone position.

In classic hammer-and-anvil doctrine, an enemy unit was being pushed toward the platoon's blocking position.

Lt. Anderson, a black West Pointer, raised up.

"Where's the fire coming from?" the lieutenant asked.

"It came from behind us," a voice answered.

Soon the firing mostly receded. With sounds of choppers somewhere in the background, the Anderson Platoon hugged the earth. An occasional bullet flew overhead.

The lieutenant raised up to peek around.

"Put your weapons on safety," he said. "All right! We gotta move."

A voice asked, "How we gonna move?"

Choppers hit the clearing to move them over to where third platoon was in trouble in an area not tropical but with wild cactus growing along a stony mountainside.

It was the front line.

THOOP! A GI raised quickly, firing a grenade launcher. He got down quickly.

THOOP! Again. **THOOP!** The GI "walked" the bomblets, and they exploded farther away each time in a straight line.

He got down for protection, then jumped up again.

THOOP!

Two Americans were killed and several badly wounded.

The platoon stood up, two at a time, and ran forward under covering fire toward the enemy position. Bulked down by equipment, each pair of soldiers trudged ahead under fire almost in slow-motion. Clumsy and awkward under the weight. Not the nimble battlefield scat one saw in Audie Murphy movies.

Reece got pounded suddenly in a leg. He collapsed in place; grimacing, waiting for Medevac.

The film ended as it began: Under a cloudy lifeless sky at a mountain firebase guarded by the Anderson platoon.

The credits rolled. Only the sound of lazy artillery rounds every four or five seconds. Interdiction and harassment fire rumbling out toward the canopy below.

Boom........ Boom........ Boom........ Boom........

As much the sound of fighting in the Vietnam War as the frantic beat of chopper blades ever was.

Four months after we got back to San Diego, I was at a family picnic on a chilly Sunday evening at Wind and Sea beach. My cousin's two boys from Texas were busy digging a huge hole in the sand. A cold ocean current had come in unexpectedly. We were all bundled up in sweaters except for the two lads who seemed impervious.

From my beach chair, I complimented them on digging a first-rate "fighting hole."

The older of the two would be in the ninth grade next year.

He asked, "What's that?"

His dad, my cousin, told them that they had dug a foxhole, which was deep enough that they could almost stand up in it. M y cousin then glanced around warily. "If the *Jerry's* ever invade this beach, you boys'll be ready for 'em!"

"What are Jerry's, Dad?" the younger boy asked.

I piped in: "Nazee Huns, dude. Germans!"

This precipitated a discussion of war. I pointed out that Uncle Jake, standing only yards away, had been in Vietnam as a Marine. The boys started asking me questions about what he did, did he ever fire his gun, and so forth.

Since Jake had been there and I hadn't, I was uneasy answering for him, but the discussion turned to war movies. Much to my surprise, the two kids had seen almost every one of them. They rattled off the names.

I suggested that my cousin pick up a tape of *The Anderson Platoon*. It was realistic; not a Hollywood production.

The ninth grader asked, "What about *Platoon*? That's my

favorite one. That wasn't realistic, either?"

Smugly, I said, "Nope."

The boys looked crestfallen. As soon as I said it, my cousin started to open his mouth then held back. In other words, he had decided to wait until they got back to the condo to tell the kids how Uncle Harry was full of crap.

Petite and I got home later that night after dark. I started thinking about the conversation on the beach. It was disconcerting for several reasons. Here I was: assuming the role of the big "expert," and gullible kids were swallowing it up, even though I had never been there during the war. Also I had to question whether what I had spouted on about bore any resemblance to the truth.

After all, *Platoon* was an Oliver Stone production. And he had been there, surely some of the scenes were very realistic.

However, Hollywood was by its nature, entertainment. It could not make a truly realistic war movie because war was, for the most part, boring.

It was chilly on the beach that evening. I should have told the kids that being in the field could be sitting on hard ground in cold rain under a wet poncho, eating C-rations, trying to stay warm, and really not doing anything else. That it could go on for weeks during the rainy season. That mail call might be the most exciting thing that occurred at these times.

That war was miserable, neither glorious nor exciting for the most part. That in movies the characters were interesting or it wouldn't be a good movie. In the real army, not so.

And that even time in combat, not boring, was never portrayed by Hollywood as it was in *The Anderson Platoon*. The enemy was seldom visible. Fellow soldiers were mangled and killed by the load. Mass confusion. Hysteria. Acts of both heroism and cowardice. Almost everything in between.

You, the reader, are humping sixty pounds of equipment up a jungle trail in a hundred degrees. The pilgrim, your friend twenty steps in front of you, gets his foot taken off by a land mine explosion. Everybody stops.

You scream, "Medic!"

He is in shock, drooling, his blood running in rivers.

You get a tarp around him. He is heavy.

You wonder, **Why am I here?**

An hour later, you and the other squad members are pouring sweat, trudging up the mountain again.

Swatting off mosquitoes, you have an ill foreboding.

I am next...

Which must be why I am here.

"AU REVOIR, GUNGA MINH"

Along the road to Phu Bai airport south of Hue, Minh the River was telling a story of two prostitutes. Rainy, Sunday morning, the streets wet and slick, he kept taking his eyes off the road. Eyes so shiny I began to wonder if our driver had been popping caps of mescaline. I cursed him silently for lying about the drugs.

Minh said that the girls were from Saigon. They were with two Korean businessmen who had booked a round trip to Nha Trang. The two girls with them had never been north of Saigon. Both had cameras. Away from the city, they suddenly screamed at him to stop the van a couple of times. He would skid to a halt thirty yards down the pavement and listen while they cursed him for ruining their "fucking pictures."

He took them to lunch at the same place we stopped in Phan Thiet. He ate alone. By late afternoon the demand to stop had been repeated several times. In arid Champa country four hours out of Phan Thiet, they demanded he halt once again. The two were calling Minh a "worthless, snake-bitten piece of shit."

All four passengers stepped out of the van for a group photo along the highway. They moved down the road and started to pose. Minh was supposed to snap the camera.

But he hopped back in, pulled out, and turned around. He stopped to toss their baggage out a hundred yards down the road, and started back to Saigon without getting paid.

He said it was *really* fun. Looking in the rear view mirror.

"Good for you," I said.

He giggled.

Then I screamed, "STOP HERE NOW!"

He laughed. The van didn't slow until he turned off Highway One into Phu Bai.

Phu Bai was a former home for thirteen months to The Straight Arrow, a friend in Berlin who had been assigned in both places at an ASA field station. He was a "ditty-bopper," whose mission was to locate enemy positions by direction finding radio equipment.

I had always gotten the impression from The Straight Arrow that he had been sitting right atop the DMZ, albeit surrounded by Marines. Yet Phu Bai was close to the coast, over a hundred miles from the DMZ. The Straight Arrow was not above straying from the absolute truth if it made a better story.

He had been rocketed a couple of times at Phu Bai during his tenure there. He told these tales in his funny, Southern accent; the humor based on helplessness in a random situation.

"Too damn random" was how he put it.

As we drove through Phu Bai, a military base as well as an airport, it reminded me of a virgin Houston. Pine forests, heavy air.

We were in the middle of the country of Vietnam here at Phu Bai, yet this was considered the far north in the American days. It was only halfway up the S-curve.

We got out of the van at a dinky airport terminal, and somehow managed to part company with Minh without severe emotional trauma. I promised to send him pictures. We hoped to see him again some day.

I was in the lounge, looking at two sparkling airplanes on the tarmac. Both were Vietnam Airlines jets going to Hanoi thirty minutes apart. We were booked on the second one.

I was hoping the cold had turned for the better up in Hanoi, when I spotted the American fellow from the *Ong Tao* restaurant the night before. He walked up and introduced himself.

He said, "I would have come over and talked to you last night but I thought you were Australian."

Whatever.

"You have such a tan," he added.

I introduced him to Petite. "This is Bob, he's from Ohio."

Bob told me he had served as a Major during the war here in Hue. He asked me if I had been in Vietnam at that time, thinking I had been.

I told him I put in my four years as an enlisted man in Berlin, a Spec-4. In other words, a Corporal. "Hitler's old rank."

He asked whether I knew Colonel So-And-So who had been in Berlin in the 1960s.

I said, "I didn't know many Colonels. And thank god they didn't know me either."

He put a hand on my shoulder in a fatherly manner, though we were close to the same age.

Bob said, "We were all enlisted men once, you know."

I supposed he had read this statement in an officer's guidebook. However, the novel concept started my mind racing to compute the probability. It did seem that everyone went through basic training. Perhaps it was true.

He said, "Know, Harry. You ought to give us a break."

I told him it was great that he came back, and that I admired the fact that he had volunteered for duty in Vietnam.

He was traveling with another former Major, a buddy. This fellow was quite tall, with the most distinctive French nose I've seen since Charles de Gaulle. Bob hauled him over and introduced him. Their story was that they had returned to Hue, the scene of a furious battle in which they had fought. They had arranged to meet the former NVA Major who directed the other side, now living in Hue.

The ex-warriors got together, hashed it out, and relived the donnybrook. It was a successful reunion of former enemies.

I was eager to hear about it, but they were on the first flight and it was boarding. We exchanged addresses. Bob didn't mention which side had won the battle and I didn't ask. I supposed the Americans had.

In a warm mist, Petite and I strolled on the tarmac toward the airplane. I wore a Luau shirt and jeans with no precaution for chilly weather, remembering a girl along the way in Nha Trang who had giggled, pointed, and called me, "Movie Star."

I can't remember how they managed fit my swelled head through the front door. But somehow they did.

We were on our way to North Vietnam.

THE NORTH

"TRUMAN SHOW"

We landed just past eleven a.m. at Noi Bai airport north of Hanoi. Down the airplane steps and onto the cement runway, a blast of cold wind hit me ill prepared. I scuffled along into the terminal. It was 54 degrees Fahrenheit, but it was a wet 54, and we had been in the tropics for two weeks.

Inside the terminal we were attacked by men-in-black, official taxi drivers. I pretended they weren't really there and walked to the baggage ramp. These drivers were a hard looking bunch. My first impression was that we had landed in Korea.

Petite had meanwhile engaged a shy, gentle young man among the pack of aggressive hounds. We got outside to his taxi after we picked up our luggage. In no time we were on the best road I saw in Vietnam, a four-lane freeway from Noi Bai to Hanoi. There weren't even any bicycles on it.

The view to either side was bright green fields against the gloom of the horizon, a delta.

Petite talked to the driver in Vietnamese, then she turned and told me that he had said that I must have been handsome when I was young.

I was curious.

"So that means I'm not handsome now, right?"

She conferred with the driver.

"No, he says you're very handsome now."

I said, "Remind me to leave him a handsome tip."

"He told me I look so young," Petite said.

Another airport-taxi whizzed by on our left. Up ahead it slowed, approaching a van that now moved into the left lane, blocking the way at 40 mph. The taxi driver sat on the horn, but the van didn't give way. The taxi started to pull to the right lane and the van swerved immediately, blocking it again.

Petite and I wondered about that.

Our driver explained that it was an Army van. The soldiers were bored, and they were playing games with the driver in front of us. Finally the army let us both past. I looked over. The troops were laughing, having a jolly time on Sunday morning with hardly any traffic on the freeway. A cheap thrill.

It took about thirty minutes to get into town.

Petite asked the driver, "Do people in Hanoi dislike Americans?"

The driver laughed loudly, as if to say, "*How silly!*"

"No," he said. "Hanoi people like Americans!"

Per my request, Petite asked, "Do people in Hanoi dislike Southerners?"

He got a bit pensive. "No," he said.

It sounded like the Party line.

Petite turned and told me in English that Northerners were much more reserved, and that they probably would not say what they really thought, anyway.

We turned our attention to the immediate problem, which was deciding where to tell the driver to take us. We had not picked out a hotel. I scrambled through the **Rough Guide**, cursing myself for putting it off so long until I came to:

"*Hotel Eden: An unusual palm-house atrium and quality wood furnishings give a touch of character to this efficient business hotel. Downstairs is a good cafe-style restaurant and popular bar.*"

It was three blocks south of Hoan Kiem Lake in the middle of Hanoi's French district. The lake was central to the tourist area.

Even on the outskirts of the city we passed French-style

buildings with old orange walls. Into town, we first saw Hanoi's elegant, shaded boulevards, with riders bundled up against the weather on their bicycles. Buzzing along a wide city street, I spotted a girl with a slogan printed across her windbreaker jacket.

The American Dream, it said.

The streets were crazy, as in Europe, coming in and joining from different directions. The deeper into the center of town we got, the more Hanoi began to look like Paris. It was the cleanest pavement I had seen in Vietnam. Like San Diego.

Minh the River had lied out the ying-yang. That was apparent. The wood fish must have been baloney, too.

Why?

He knew I would find out the truth!

Our taxi pulled up to the Hotel Eden and stopped on a narrow street. My Chief Negotiator disembarked, along with the cabby.

Remaining behind with our luggage, I found it disconcerting to sit in the back seat with the window rolled down, smoking a cigarette, looking out on the busy street and realizing that not one person walking or riding by was paying a bit of attention to me.

A return to anonymity. This was different.

I started to miss all the fuss.

Petite later told me that within months after the end of the fighting in 1975, there was a mass tourist migration to the North. She said that even the cooks and bottle-washers took off for a couple of weeks' visit. Most Southerners had relatives in North Vietnam they had not seen for years. Petite said her mother had gone up then to visit long-lost cousins.

Though the Communist North had won, it was devastated. Uneven electric power. Extreme poverty. Most of what the Southern people saw of the living conditions made them scoff.

They returned home with tales, many of which were true at the time. Most of the Southerners never trooped back north again. They had seen it with their own eyes. Minh the River, especially, seemed to enjoy spinning these yarns.

But, my, time did change things.

I wrote in my diary about our first day in Hanoi:

"This is the most beautiful city in Asia."

I sprawled on a double bed. Room 22 at the Hotel Eden. An NCAA basketball tournament game was on color television. Live - in English with the American announcers on Rupert Murdoch's cable station. Not exactly what I had expected I would be doing in Hanoi.

I liked it.

At each break in the action, two Chinese basketball players on the national team came on the screen as moderators. They spoke either Mandarin or Cantonese. The only intelligible words were "Kentucky" and "Duke."

Petite picked up the phone. She dialed Auntie Giang, whom she had never met before. Auntie Giang and Uncle Ky had grown up in Quang Ngai province in the South. In 1954 the country was partitioned and Giang was the only member of the family to elect to move north, as she and her husband were idealistic college students who sympathized with the Viet Minh.

Her husband Ky had become a diplomat for North Vietnam. I was told that he spoke English, and enjoyed arguing. I had some questions, and was looking forward to a little verbal sparring.

Petite hung up the phone and said that Auntie Giang was on the way over. It would take about thirty minutes by bus.

Auntie Giang knocked on the door, as the buzzer sounded ending the basketball game. Kentucky won in the last seconds to move to the Final Four the next weekend.

Petite greeted her relative, who was a happy looking woman in her sixties, dressed in a raincoat.

We headed down the stairs and into the Pear Tree Bar on the ground floor of the hotel. There were a dozen customers when we arrived; half Vietnamese, half foreign. The Pear Tree Bar had a pub decor with two pool tables. Best of all it had a menu with Western food. The Vietnamese clientele was young; one couple sat across from us sharing a pizza.

An older Aussie ex-pat was chatting loudly with two Aussie surfer-types with backpacks who had just arrived in Hanoi, filling them in on what to do in town. The kids never got in a word edgewise.

I could hear every word the man said, while I looked at the menu.

Everyone in the bar seemed to be surreptitiously checking out everyone else, except for Petite and Giang rattling away in Vietnamese and oblivious to anyone else including me. They seemed to be hitting it off.

I decided to order Chili Con Carne.

From the next table: "...Yer can see *Bac Ho*, Uncle Ho, that's Ho Chi Minh, mates. Got 'im lyed out in a mausoleum just down the way eah," the ex-pat said.

I now noticed they had three clear bottles of beer on the table. Corona!

I looked it up on the menu. Three dollars. That may have been outrageous by Vietnamese standards, but not much more than it would cost at a nice bar in Tijuana.

Someone switched the background music from Reggae to Live Nirvana, "Unplugged in New York."

"... got 'im lyed out like a mackerel," the Aussie announced, referring to Uncle Ho.

Petite grabbed my arm, excited.

"Guess what?" she said. "I'm related to a King through my father's side, too! I never knew that! I thought it was only Mother's side."

Auntie Giang confirmed the news in limited English.

The kids at the pool tables, and the couple eating pizza, as well as the Vietnamese employees behind the bar, were now all looking at us. Not being coy about it, either. We were now the center of attention.

Petite turned to Auntie Giang. She began a loud conversation in Vietnamese, no doubt about the royal family.

The Aussie at the next table turned up the volume. "Take you lads to Madame Nhu's. Got some Sheilas down there. Bang like a shithouse door in a gale, give 'em a fair shake."

But no one else gave a damn. They were all listening to Petite and Auntie.

I had not uttered one word since the waitress took our order what seemed like hours ago when I said "thank you" in Vietnamese. Sitting there, I thought how most of the Americans I had met in Vietnam had ended up with the same disease after a week's time. The disease of hubris, manifested by loud, authoritative dissertations in public places, without considering that others in hearing range could possibly be disinterested.

Offshoots of this were vanity, self-importance, and egomania. I was ill equipped to be immune. I was a writer. But until Hanoi I hadn't realized how infected I had gotten in two short weeks.

When the Chili Con Carne came out to the table, it was piping hot. I put extra cheese on top. Spicy.

Dynamite Mexican grub.

Viva Hanoi!

"FULL SAIL"

Back in the room, I turned on the television to CNN.

The news lady was talking about a pair of high-school kids in Jonesboro, Arkansas, who had ambushed and gunned down several school chums. The story of the hour.

Ho hum.

Auntie was downstairs in the lobby. We were going to take a taxi to her house to meet Uncle Ky.

I tried to pick out a shirt that didn't reek.

Sweating wasn't a problem here.

Auntie Giang's neighborhood was elegant and wooded. The elderly couple lived behind a gate and courtyard in a two-story house. She ushered us into the den and went to find Uncle Ky.

I gazed at a large fish tank.

Back at the restaurant Giang had made a point to tell us that she was "non-political." She had merely followed her husband to the North.

Smiling, Ky appeared with willowy white hair. He offered Petite and I a choice of coffee or tea. Three of us sat down in a small den, while Auntie went to the kitchen to boil water.

He told us that they had cable television there at home, the same as at the hotel. He, too, liked CNN. When I asked how much it cost, he said it was about ten dollars a month.

Following the obligatory small talk, which was in English, Giang came back in carrying a tray with cups and saucers.

I attempted to strike up meaningful discourse, mentioning to Ky that we had stopped over at My Lai on the way up. Rather than provoke comment, this approach seemed to embarrass him. It had been a selfish move on my part.

I studied the fish tank for a good while through a cup of coffee. The three of them were speaking Vietnamese. Finally I got bored and walked out to the courtyard to smoke.

Outside was a pretty patio, red bougainvillea. I noticed that the bottoms of my jeans were muddy.

Pacing around puffing the cigarette, I heard a faint bell tinkling behind the cute gate to the street. After wandering over and peeking through the mail slot, I saw a man bending over who looked like "Bac Ho," white beard and all. He held out a cup. I presumed it was for food and that he was a neighborhood regular. He did not seem surprised to see the big white stranger behind the gate.

I slid a 1,000 into his bowl through the slot.

Back inside the others were still refusing to include me in the conversation. Figuring it would be a tough row to hoe, I adjourned to the bathroom to sort it out.

Surprise. Giang had put American fixtures in the downstairs head, which was more than I could say for our hotel. I spent some time in front of the mirror; finally convincing myself it was now or never. Go on. Be a creepy guest.

Let go the rigging. Damn the torpedoes. Full sail ahead.

Back in the den, I waited to pounce on the first pause in conversation. It finally came, as it always did.

I said, "The reason I mentioned that we went to My Lai was to let you know why. Americans realize that things happened that we weren't exactly proud of. But the constant communist propaganda in Saigon museums got a bit tiresome. Know what I mean? Seemed a tad hypocritical. And I have to tell you, the most disappointing situation I've come across in Vietnam is that children must pay to get a basic education. I mean, that prevents half the kids in the countryside from having a chance in life. And this is a Communist society?"

I was a little embarrassed after it came out. I had not meant to sound so much like Jimmy Swaggert.

Uncle Ky nodded his head. He agreed that education was important and that it was too bad school could not be free of charge. He said, "It used to be free until *doi moi*. Now people have to pay for *everything*."

He said it as a matter of fact, implying that it wasn't his idea, anyway. It was the nasty economic reform policy that was to blame.

Of course it was. Sure.

If Fidel's Cuba could afford free education, anyone could.

But I didn't say that. Uncle Ky was a little hard of hearing, at any rate. Retired for several years, he had lost some influence, we had been told. Although no longer allowed to travel out of the country together as a couple, they represented the privileged class in Communist society. The diplomatic corps had been a meritocracy. Ky had not achieved success without hard work. He had been in Paris at times during the negotiations to end the war. Possibly he knew too much for his own good.

I was itching to ask Giang and Ky if they had ever heard of the massacre at Hue. But these were matters they did not want to discuss, so I decided to be polite, for a change.

The issue concerning Hue was to try to find out to what extent history could be rewritten in the information age.

Ky showed the first sign of emotion when I asked him if he had been in Hanoi during the bombing by the B52s. He talked about the air raids and the sirens, how he spent a lot of time in bomb shelters. Several thousand civilians were killed, including some in a hospital. Auntie Giang and the two kids had been sent out into the countryside. Ky was alone in Hanoi.

After a week, he got worried about the family. The raids became less intensive, so he took off on his bicycle to where Giang was.

At this point in his story, Uncle looked over to Auntie seated across the table.

She giggled like a schoolgirl.

He said, "Along a road out of Hanoi I met Giang, coming the other way. She had been worried about me, too. *I'll never forget that moment.* I was so happy."

By the time we finished up at their home it was dark.

Four of us piled into a cab to a local restaurant. It was misty outside, a cool evening. The road was shiny, slick from a recent sprinkle. Streetlight shimmered off the pavement as we raced along. The taxi pulled up near the shore of Hoan Kiem Lake.

Walking up a stairwell, we passed by a group of boys in a karate classroom. The restaurant balcony overlooked the lake with a great view of the shining, lighted Tortoise Tower sitting on its own little island.

Before we went inside, I lingered to take in the misty night-time scene again, feeling as if it were someplace in Central Europe.

Throughout an overpriced meal, Ky and I never spoke directly to one another. Because he and Giang did not know me, my pickiness about Vietnamese food probably turned them off. The Vietnamese were abnormally interested in whether you liked their cuisine or not.

I tried to grab the bill and pay the tab, but Auntie Giang snatched it out of my grasp like a cobra.

Afterwards, we all got into a taxi, which first dropped off Petite and I at our hotel. I slipped the cab driver 50,000 dong to cover the entire trip, for them as well, and his tip, although Giang was furiously protesting from the back seat.

The taxi pulled away. Petite seemed upset for some reason.

"What's the deal?" I asked.

She shook her head, the you-are-so-stupid look.

"You should have let Auntie pay! That was very rude."

"Huh?"

"Listen, the custom here is that if you invite someone to go somewhere, you have to pay for everything. If you can't afford to do that, then don't invite 'em. You *seemed* to be *insinuating* they couldn't pay, or something. If they want to pay for something, let 'em pay!"

"SOR-RRY."

"Guess you didn't mean to," she sniffed.

It was news to me that I had been so insulting.

"You know," I said, "that's one problem we never had with Uncle down in Saigon."

"SOLDIERS OF THE WAR"

It was two months after we returned to San Diego, when HBO showed *A Bright Shining Lie*, a movie based on the book by Neil Sheehan. The network billed the protagonist of the story, Lt. Colonel John Paul Vann, as "The Soldier of the War" in Vietnam.

John Paul Vann served in country for eight years from 1962-1963, and from 1965-1972. He was there at the beginning of the American involvement, as well as toward the end.

The movie was accurate and true to the book in most instances. However, it had a fatal flaw. Vann was a consummate warrior, thrilling to an occasional battle. He took awful risks and seemed fearless to his contemporaries. He seemed to have a death wish, yet he was never seriously wounded.

The real Vann was a born leader and an intelligent man, but he was short of stature. The HBO movie presented a tall fellow in the part, and it seemed to me that this detracted from reality in the sense that his lines in the movie were delivered as man who was six-foot-two would deliver them. As for Vann's actual presence, I imagined that he was similar to fellow iconoclast, Ross Perot.

Vann was patriotic. He never questioned the propriety of the American effort in Vietnam, although his colleague and friend, Daniel Ellsberg, later did. Vann was an early critic of how the war was being fought. He was most concerned with corruption in the South Vietnamese government and military, compounded by the ignorance of the American military's upper echelon, who had convinced themselves that they were fighting the Battle of the Bulge over again.

Vietnam was not the first time. The lesson of Korea should have been that Western armies could not win a war of attrition in

Asia.

Edward Lansdale had been Vann's guiding light. Early on, Vann co-opted the theory that the key to success was the Southern peasantry - that is, improving the government, training its army to respect the people, and providing U.S. aid in the countryside to win over the populace. His early career in Vietnam was spent as an irritating thorn in the side of conventional wisdom.

Had it not been for the American presence, the Communists would have taken over by 1965. Our efforts prolonged the inevitable for a decade. The end was inevitable due to the wholesale corruption of the Southern leadership. The many instances of rotten spore at the top of the chain were pointed out in Neil Sheehan's book. The massive inflow of American dollars encouraged it, as well. Ironically, the Communist government that followed has had to deal with a similar Mandarin vestige; the ability of the governing class to profit heavily.

Nevertheless, Vann was an optimist. He held out hope on the day he died in a crash in 1972 that the South would somehow prevail, albeit with an American air shield. This was a direct result of the amount of time and effort he had invested in the cause.

Vann was a true ex-patriot. He got an early taste of the so-called "exotic little war" in 1962, when the VC would avoid targeting Americans for fear of arousing the stateside public. It seemed to me that he never felt comfortable living in America after he had experienced Vietnam. He was an insatiable womanizer, the conqueror-male personality type, who happened to be alienated from his parents.

Vann wore many hats in Vietnam - military advisor, U.S. aid official and civilian military attaché. He saw many of the war's battles from the air in a scout chopper, and was involved in several on the ground. In 1972 he directed B-52 attacks against the NVA. With few exceptions, he and the journalists who idolized him seemed to consider the ARVN as cowardly, when in fact leadership was the problem, not the common foot soldier, who was poorly trained and as the American GIs, improperly deployed in a war of attrition.

One of the old wives tales that was heard over and again in both the U.S. and Vietnam was that if the Americans had only invaded the North, the outcome would have been different.

There were four good reasons for why this was not true.

1) The NVA had the will to fight on forever, as well as the means - an arms supply from China and Russia.

2) The terrain was the most favorable for guerrilla warfare that I have ever seen; a tropical Afghanistan.

3) The point was moot to begin with, as the entire American strategy was to avoid bringing China into the conflict, which an invasion of the North, if anything, would have precipitated.

4) The Southern government never had the will to do what it took to win - that is, reform its institutions.

An Achilles heel in U.S. policy: The last thing anyone in Washington wanted to do was to set up an outright American colony. Simply put, this conflicted with the American self image, and its stated goals.

However, in retrospect, the only way the Communist victory could have remotely been avoided would have been to set up a MacArthur-style American governor with imperial power to root out corruption with prison terms for the offenders. To start over again at the top and hope to create a new society. Although historically this should not have worked, either, Vann figured it was the best chance for success. Like MacArthur, he certainly wanted the job.

That John Paul Vann had been designated "Soldier of the War" in Vietnam was an example of Yankee myopia. To my recollection, such distinctions were normally reserved for a player on the *winning* side.

Some might say that NVA General Vo Nguyen Giap deserved the accolade "Soldier of the War."

I disagree.

He was a general.

Generals were not, nor have they ever been "soldiers."

Giving John Paul Vann his due, this case called for a dual award. In my opinion, the co-winner was author Bao Ninh: The common NVA enlisted man, as seen through his character, Kien, in **The Sorrow of War**.

Kien's impressions of the war in Vietnam were a bit different than Lt. Colonel Vann's.

"Kien had perhaps watched more killings and seen more corpses than any other contemporary writer. He had seen rows of youthful American soldiers, their bodies unscathed, leaning shoulder to shoulder in trenches and dugouts, sleeping an everlasting sleep because artillery barrages had blocked their exit, sucking life from them. Parachutists still in their camouflaged uniforms lying near bushes around a landing zone in the Ko Leng forest, burning in the hot noonday sun, with only hawks above and flies below to covet their bodies. And a rain of arms and legs dropping before him onto the grass by the Sa Thay River during a night raid by B-52s. Hamburger Hill after three days of bloody fighting, looking like a domed roof built with corpses. A soldier stepping onto a mine and being blown to the top of a tree, as if he had wings... Kien's soldiers came from beyond the grave and told of their lives beyond death."

Perhaps the most important way that Kien and Vann were alike was that they both became what they originally hated.

As a disciple of Lansdale, it must have been incongruous

even to Vann himself that, by the end, he was calling in the B-52s. Kien found himself in situations where he executed enemy soldiers.

About the only other thing they had in common as well as being skilled soldiers, was that both were from what we would now call "broken homes."

Kien was from an intellectual family. He was estranged from his father, an artist who painted only in yellows. Kien's closest "relative" was a stepfather, a poet, and he hardly knew his mother.

Vann's mother was reputedly a prostitute. His father was a run-of-the-mill lowlife.

That was pretty much where the resemblance between John Paul Vann and Kien ended.

Kien was the product of a gentler society, one in which most of the young men seemed to worship women, or at the very least, treat them as sisters. There were many women soldiers in the NVA forces, as well.

Kien enjoyed sitting by a mountain stream smoking rosa canina, fishing with a handline in the rain.

Vann preferred the carnal pleasures on his time off.

Vann seemed almost to believe that he was immortal, and he was only superficially wounded while alive.

Bao Ninh naturally figured to die at any time, but he was one of ten survivors of the original 500 members of the Glorious 27th Youth Brigade in 1969.

"Kien waited for death, calmly recognizing that it would be ugly and inelegant. The thought of his expected end brought a sense of irony."

Kien was wounded severely several times, and spent time in the field hospital.

"And down the bank and along the stream Kien dragged himself, bleeding from the mouth and from his body wound. The

191

blood was cold and sticky, like blood from a corpse. Snakes and centipedes crawled over him, and he felt death's hand on him."

It read almost like The Bible.

I came to believe that Americans failed to understand how different the North was from the South, as well as how much the Northern people, especially its soldiers, suffered during the war.

Americans were the ones with air power: scout choppers, Hueys, F-4 Phantoms, B-52s.

A number of times in Vietnam we passed a playground and I saw tiny jet planes attached to the swings and merry-go-rounds. Hardly a single museum in Saigon did not sport at least a rusted F-4 on its front lawn.

Kien got his first taste of the bombing on a train with his girl friend Phuong on the way south to try to catch up with a troop train he had missed after basic training. The Americans entered the war full-scale just as he graduated from high school, so Kien had patriotically volunteered for the Army.

The horror of bombing could produce unintended consequences.

"It had been sheer coincidence that Phuong had been on the train at all. She had wanted to go as far as possible with Kien to the front, with no concern for the consequences.

There had been two raids. The first, a shorter one was when the train had been forced to stop. Kien had been knocked unconscious and flung into an embankment. He was dazed. He hadn't been able to recognize which car he'd been in, and when attempting to get back on the train he had missed his footing several times and got more injuries.

Now he dimly recalled dreaming some ugly scenes; they came to him in contrasting black-and-white images, like negatives on film. Still bleeding and dizzy, he had scrambled onto the locomotive as the train started off again and fallen into a deep sleep."

The train headed south again for Vinh, next to the DMZ. It stopped in the morning at Thanh Hoa city station. Kien awoke. He got out of the railroad car and saw that the station was now leveled - a field of craters.

A drunken sailor stumbled out of the railroad car behind him.

"The big man was about thirty years old. He had a large, square face with a moronic forehead, a squat, fat nose, and a thick chin, and he smiled with a cruel leer. He stared aggressively. Under the striped sailor's shirt his hard muscles bulged."

Kien climbed into the railroad car, looking for Phuong.

He found his virgin love of several years laid across a stack of rice sacks in the back.

"Phuong couldn't answer. Instead she shook her head, then looked down.

Kien began to close her blouse but there wasn't a single button left. Her bare breasts were covered with a cold film of sweat. Kien felt himself unable to cope or to understand fully what had happened. He began to cry painful, salty tears which hotly ran down his cheeks, and he almost choked as he tried to comfort her with more words."

Kien spent the next eleven years in the NVA, most of it as the leader of the scout platoon; the forward element. He distrusted officers and their constant propaganda rallies. Once he and a group of his friends spent several days at a prosperous Southern plantation in the Central Highlands, and were in awe of the good life they witnessed, amazed by the abundance.

"Driving away from the plantation in the late afternoon, no one spoke for some minutes. Finally, Van, who had been a university student in economics, started to speak: 'There, you see. That's the way to live! What a peaceful, happy oasis. My lecturers

*with all their Marxist theories will pour in and ruin all this if we win. I'm horrified to think what will happen to that couple. They'll soon learn what the term **new political order** means.'*

Another replied, 'Damn right they'll be unhappy. If we do win and return after the war, I wonder if they'll still treat us kindly.'

'Not unless you come back as the chairman of the new cooperative!' Van laughed.

But the thought had appalled them, and when Van spoke again he was somber: 'That will be sad, really. I wonder if my own district will ever develop such lovely farms. Our landscape at Moc Chau is similar to this, yet we're always so poor.'"

It took a grand pair of *cajones* to write the above and publish it in Vietnam, something Vann would have admired.

Most of Kien's experiences diametrically opposed his government's official story, especially when he recounts the courage of Saigon soldiers, even as all was lost.

The most crunching disappointment for Kien was the war's aftermath. No congratulations awaited from civilian Hanoi when he returned home. The city had changed from his youth, and the economy took decades to improve. Cynicism and pessimism flooded the country. The government failed to provide support for its former soldiers, or even the war widows.

It had all been in vain, Kien thought.

Two soldiers. One war. Same result.

They both thought they had lost.

"TEMPLE OF LITERATURE"

On Monday we explored Hanoi by foot and by cyclo.

The cyclos held two people comfortably as opposed to the ones in the south, where it was too hot to peddle a big load.

Out the hotel in the morning, Petite and I bundled up. I had on a windbreaker. She needed her sweater. In my diary I described the weather: *"Cool, not quite chilly but close: Misty."*

The streets were slick, as usual, with standing pools of water on the sidewalks. These required a skip around. Even with a decent map, the layout of the city confused me. We got lost or went way out of the way several times in four days.

Three blocks from our hotel, I guided us to what had to be the "Hanoi Hilton," as it was known in America; an old prison where U.S. pilots were jailed. Among the former POWs were the current Ambassador to Vietnam, Pete Peterson, as well as one U.S. Senator I considered as more than an empty suit and phony grin, John McCain of Arizona.

I had expected to see a massive prison, but a modern skyscraper rose from most of the original site and dominated everything else. It was the tallest building I saw in Hanoi. The government had preserved a portion of the old jails, which did not appear to us as open to the public.

Petite took a photo of the orange wall and guard tower.

We headed up a boulevard, lined with trees, toward the next stop, the Temple of Literature. As we walked, I struggled to decipher the map, as well as to search for shortcuts. The street names for the same road seemed to change every other block.

Petite pointed out how European it all seemed.

We gave up and asked a shopkeeper along the way for directions. I instructed Petite to translate, "Temple of Literature."

She did that and came away with a blank stare from the storekeeper, who then asked me to point it out on my map.

We were going the right direction. They did not call it "The Temple of Literature."

Okay.

We were close, I could get there without a map now.

When I finally got to look at the scenery, Hanoi seemed cosmopolitan; at least in the French district where we were. It was a little gloomy but in a romantic way. The type of place, you could stroll along humming a Frank Sinatra song and feel at home.

"Those Autumn leaves..."

Saigon was not like that at all.

Petite said, "This is a good transition to San Diego."

She was right.

This was a Vietnam we had not known; seeming more hybrid. More like should I say, America? People on the streets weren't staring, or even bothering us to buy something. We never felt as if we'd zoomed into town off a flying saucer.

Hearty, life-sustaining Western food was readily available.

It was **chilly** outside.

There were a number of Famous Artists in Hanoi, I was sure. Petite knew not one of them. Most of the relatives spoke English. They wanted to pay for everything because we were guests.

It was like a different country.

And a delightful change: Not as I expected.

Known as *Van Mieu*, the shaded ground of the Temple of Literature and National University was a significant cultural vestige of Vietnam. Of Hanoi, especially, because Van Mieu lay at the center of the original town settlement.

The temple building was first erected in 1070. There were statues of Confucius, as well as of his four best pupils, or disciples. Paintings of 72 other Confucian scholars were part of the original monument. Six years later in 1076, the university was established on the site. The Crown Princes studied here.

From the **Rough Guide**: *"Becoming A Mandarin"*

"Examinations for admission to the imperial bureaucracy were introduced by the kings in the eleventh century. Vietnam's exams were based on the Chinese system, although included were Buddhist and Taoist texts.

It took until the fifteenth century for academic success, rather than noble birth or patronage, to become the primary means of entry to the civil service. By this time the system was open to all males, excluding 'traitors, rebels, immoral people and actors,' but in fact very few candidates outside the scholar-gentry class progressed beyond the lowest possible rung.

The national exam might last up to six weeks and was as much an evaluation of poetic style and knowledge of the classic texts as it was of administrative ability. Those who passed were granted a doctorate and made eligible for the final test, the palace exam, set by the king himself.

Some years as few as three would be rewarded, of the 6,000 who originally took the regional exams. Afterwards, the king would give his new mandarins a cap, gown, parasol and a horse on which to return to their home-village in a triumphal procession.

In 1947, French bombs destroyed the academy buildings, leaving a few traces visible among the weeds."

A sailor's dead reckoning was always the best method. We located the correct city block and followed a colored brick wall to a two-tier gate, where I paid the entrance fee.

As usual Petite got in free. She was my "guide."

Past the attendant big oak trees shaded a grassy courtyard, and we had the choice of a left or right walkway. We took the right pathway. In the shade of oak leaves I glanced at the wall, feeling secure from the vicious outside world.

Into a second walled courtyard, a film crew was training the spotlights on four radiating suns carved onto a wooden second-story facade.

In the next area we saw a moat-shaped pond with murky brown water smothered by lily paddies.

I paused, referencing the guidebook.

Ah, yes...

"The Well of Heavenly Clarity."

Of course.

Petite went on ahead.

I gazed into the pond searching for answers to great unknowns. Was my kitty at home going to die soon? Soon an acorn bounced off my baseball cap.

I looked up. A squirrel.

The grounds were laid out according to Confucius's birthplace in China. In the next courtyard there was a building on each side. 82 stele mounted on huge stone tortoises faced the center of the courtyard, recording the names of students who passed the National Academy examinations from 1442 onward.

A brochure I picked up at the entrance explained, *"The erection of the stele and engraving of the names of **doctors to laureate** under different dynasties were aimed at encouraging and showing honor to the talented men."*

These commemorations began fifty years before Columbus set off for the Indies to see what was "behind the weather." The actual examinations began about the time of William the Conqueror in England. Even today, it was only the North, which produced such world-class institutions as the Institute of Mathematics in Hanoi.

We strolled past a lonely vendor at her stand in front of the "Gate of Great Success." There appeared a courtyard, and a temple with the sound of live traditional music coming from inside. Outside on the temple steps was a woman dressed in a northern peasant costume, brilliant against the overcast day: Magenta. Yellow. Red. Black. A green sash.

She took off her hat. She offered it to Petite. The hat was similar to a wide white *sombrero* with tassels. A beaming yellow streamer hung at each side.

I snapped a picture of the two together; Petite in the hat.

With music playing from somewhere inside, I walked into the sanctuary. There seemed to be two of everything in this one. Identical wooden kings, with Fu Manchu beards, red robes, and gold helmets.

I turned, facing the altar.

At the ready, Petite manned the camera.

A pair of turquoise flamingos fronted the shrine. The birds had dinosaur-like heads, plated spines, swooping necks.

Dragon Birds, I thought, stepping into the space between the two protruding "beaks," about to execute a most reverent bow.

Hot and clear, it was a July afternoon four months later. On the redwood deck by a swimming pool in San Diego, we sat at a glass table under the turquoise umbrella.

My blond eighteen-year-old niece stopped thumbing through the photographs we took in Vietnam. Puzzled, she looked over.

I rocked back and forth in a deck chair.

She asked, *"Is that **you**?... Bowing there?"*

I coughed.

She smiled.

"Sure," I said.

She handed me the photo.

Petite had snapped it at the moment when I was in a steep bow and holding for a second beneath the dragon birds. Personal schtick. (I have ended up bowing more than I ever thought I would at the time I married an Asian). And a funny thing I noticed: A lot of Vietnamese tended to give but a weary nod when they were *supposed* to be bowing.

That reverent bend was my only outlet for trying to out-Nam the Vietnamese. I didn't do chopsticks.

"WHICH WAY TO..."

It was another half-hour by foot to the Ho Chi Minh complex where a museum, park, and mausoleum provided the attractions. I started to feel my ankle twitch while on the hike. Fortunately I had purchased a bamboo cane in the gift shop at the Temple of Literature.

As in many Asian cities, we passed by entire city blocks of small shops devoted to selling the same thing: the welding and soldering block, a block of flower shops, television-dealer block, and so forth.

We arrived at our destination at 11:30 a.m.

"That's it across the street," I told Petite. "The Ho Chi Minh Mausoleum."

Later I found out that the futuristic building I was pointing to was actually the HCM Museum. But no matter, it was all closed on Mondays. Next stop on the list: The Old Quarter.

We decided to take a cyclo. Petite spent ten minutes negotiating a price with three different drivers at the same time.

It was about a fifteen-minute ride. Well worth a couple of dollars in entertainment alone: whizzing through and about the traffic, as the driver tinkled a little bell before making each turn. *Ping.* He stopped at an intersection on the north side of Hoan Kiem Lake.

Petite got off first. She took a snapshot of him standing behind me, while in the pedicab seat I waved the cane at the camera, as if lashing out in imperial fury at some unfortunate coolie such as Petite. Climbing off, I noticed an audience of high-school girls on a nearby corner, laughing at this street theater.

The driver looked as if he were recovering from "the bends."

Possibly more tonnage than he had anticipated back at the ol' museum. He continued to struggle for oxygen.

Neither Petite nor I found the Old Quarter particularly fascinating, but we have been in Asia many times. Petite shopped. I bought and took pictures. Bright blue awnings and other resplendent shades of color contrasted nicely with the buildings.

By two p.m., a second cyclo driver had us safely in the restaurant back at Hotel Eden, where I gobbled one of the most welcomed pizzas I had ever eaten.

The **Rough Guide** read: *"Apocalypse Now, 338 Ba Trieu. Sister-establishment to the original bar in Ho Chi Minh City that's seething on Friday and Saturday nights - even though it's inconveniently located out in the southern boondocks. Dark, apocalyptic decor and great music. 7pm - late."*

I walked down the carpeted stairs at the Eden and into the lobby. Behind the front desk tonight was the lady who spoke perfect English and thought Petite was Japanese on our arrival.

I walked up to the desk, said hello, and asked her to phone a cab. Looking out the door, it was dark and damp on the street.

She smiled. "Where are you going?"

"The *Apocalypse Now* Bar."

She had never heard of it.

Having done some homework, I pulled out a map and pointed to where it was. It didn't look that far. What was the guide talking about? *"Southern boondocks?"* Ba Trieu was a major road running parallel and several blocks east of a familiar nearby street.

The lady glanced up from the map.

She said, "You won't need a taxi. You can easily walk."

Minh The River's advice passed before me. I thought about running upstairs to grab my pointy cane for a weapon.

"It's *perfectly* safe!" she said, laughing away the thought.

Petite bounced down the steps, ready to go.

Armed with the map, we set off into the night.

What we found: almost-deserted streets, little traffic. Darkish and misty.

Bao Dinh described his native city as such:

"In the streets below, scattered lights shone; the light mixing with the rain. Illumination stopped at the end of the street, marking the start of the vast lake. Swinging his vision to the right he saw the dark cloud canopies low over the familiar tiled roofs of Hanoi, although hardly any of the houses emitted light. There were no cars on the street and not a single pedestrian.

At this moment the city was so calm that one could practically hear the clouds blow over the rooftops. He thought of them as part of his life being blown away in wispy sections, leaving vast, open areas of complete emptiness, as in his own life.

The spirit of Hanoi is strongest by night, even stronger in the rain. Like now, when the whole town seems deserted, wet, lonely, and deeply sad."

It didn't make either Petite or I deeply sad. But then we were just tourists. We liked it. However, it did appear to me to be Berlin-type weather and I knew about the dangerous mental effect of long term exposure to that.

As the male in our walking party of two, I had certain obligations to perform as we made our way along Ba Trieu Street. Whenever the sidewalk in front of us was empty, I limped feebly along as an old man would with a bad ankle. I had worn my leather moccasins, which had no support. The weak ankle was biting again after only five minutes on cobbled rocks.

But whenever a couple of young men appeared, I picked up the pace, Petite in hand, trying to convey the impression "dat dey don't be messin' wid' Harry."

We found the address after thirty minutes. A lot of good it did us, the club had moved. Three young men sat around in front of the former site, which looked to be undergoing reincarnation into another nightclub. They were sufficiently non-threatening that I cut the macho bit. They informed us that the new *Apocalypse Now* Bar was not far away.

That was some relief. I didn't care about drinking, but I was desperate to buy some tee shirts that would fit a gringo.

Dumbly I looked around.

Down the street, a pair of headlights switched on.

A cab drove up and stopped.

We got in.

"Why don't you tell him?" I asked Petite, noticing how the Vietnamese seemed to be having trouble with the name. Maybe if the driver heard it pronounced with her Vietnamese accent...

She said, "We want to go to... uh, *Ako-plips* Now."

The cabby's eyes got squinty.

"*Acopolisp* Now... Aghh, uh..."

I said, "*Apoc-Lips* Now Bar," trying to be helpful but it was catching. "Apocalypse Now Bar," I managed again.

The driver scratched his head. He reached for the radio transmitter. "Say into phone!" he shouted back to me.

I spelled the name for her.

It took five minutes. The dispatcher looked it up and figured out where the place was. Naturally it was located the same direction we had walked from. Almost all the way back to the hotel, but one block farther over. At least, we could walk home from there.

The joint was almost empty, well lighted, with almost zero decoration. A lonely English tourist curled at the bar, chatting to the bartender. The music was lousy as well as deafening.

On my way to my barstool after depleting the inventory of XXL tee shirts, I noticed another foreign couple stroll through the door.

They sat at a table on the fringe of the empty dance floor. After a short while, the girl went up to the DJ and asked him to please lower the volume.

The man in the Immaculate Disc-Jockey booth cackled with a toothy sneer. Bob Segar got even louder. "Devil With The Blue Dress On," ad nausea.

Petite and I took it all in.

We, too, laughed about it.

Then we got up, saddled the horses, and rode outta Dodge.

The greater part of the next morning was spent, as was each morning in Hanoi, lounging around a table downstairs at the hotel restaurant. I read the newspaper. Petite chatted with the employees. We ate our free fried-eggs, our complimentary bacon, and drank copious amounts of gratis espresso that would cost $2 a cup after breakfast.

The waiters, waitresses and bartenders were college students. On behalf of the Mothers of America, I only wished I could report that Vietnam had already sent its best and brightest to the U.S.A. However, these kids were uniformly friendly, intelligent and inquisitive. It was sad to realize that if more of them end up in *your* school district, rest assured your own bright genius will never make Valedictorian.

Work, work, work. There went The Curve.

It was Tuesday morning, I had slept in late for the first time. I noted in my diary: "*Good night's sleep*." A rarity.

In an unshaven daze I found Petite having coffee down the stairs, talking to a twenty-something Vietnamese woman who sat at an adjoining table.

I pulled up a chair.

Her name was Kim, a *Viet Kieu*; a fellow Californian who lived in San Francisco. She explained that she worked for a private organization, which "fostered understanding between Vietnam and the United States." She had an All-American accent.

"Fostering understanding?" I asked.

She said, "Yes. Teaching people in the Hanoi government about principles of Western governmental organizations."

I was more interested in a cup of coffee at the time, so I got up to find a waitress. Still mulling the issue.

Principles? Government? It seemed they already had the mechanics down, thank you: Control the population and try to improve the economy.

When I got back, the girls were talking shopping.

Soon Kim excused herself.

While she was away, Petite told me, "You should talk to her. I told her you were a writer."

I said, "Gee thanks."

Kim returned shortly. She had some interesting bona-fides: two years living in Hanoi from 1991-1993, while doing her thesis for grad school.

She said Vietnam was much different back then, only five years ago. No one could travel the country like one did today without written itineraries, permits, and such. Also, she explained that there were many books now available in stores that had been banned since the 1940s. Her friends in the "intelligencia" were only now becoming aware of atrocities perpetrated by the Communists during the War of Liberation. Her friends were really just beginning to ask questions.

But she figured the common people in the countryside in North Vietnam neither knew, nor cared. She was glad that economic progress had not happened overnight in Vietnam. The society and economy were having difficulty absorbing the current rate of change, as it was. A sudden boom would have overwhelmed the situation, such as it did in the war years in the South, when prostitutes and cabbies made more money than doctors or professors.

I shared her point of view.

She said that young people did not care about the war, and resented older people telling them how hard they had it. The young were interested mainly in careers.

Kim started to tell about a Cambodian UN project she had worked for. The UN came in, threw out a bunch of cash and started the usual race for the roses, rather than solving problems.

She pulled out a cell phone to dial her uncle here in town. He made her check in every day. Living in San Francisco, she had forgotten about the strong family obligations here. As with Petite, Kim's older relatives dispensed unwanted advice, then got upset when it wasn't acted upon immediately.

I asked her if she thought Vietnam to be a promising place for American investment.

"Oh, sure," she said. "American brand-names are absolutely worshipped here. You can't *buy* that perception!"

Three hours later, Petite and I, mid-way on a stroll through the French district, noticed young people on motor scooters pulling up to an outdoor cafe.

We entered through a gate and sat at a table under an umbrella. It was lovely, a shaded area, with a view of the boulevard.

I glanced over at a couple swooning at the next table. They shared a cup of tea.

Liptons.

I pointed out the familiar label to Petite.

"Yuck!" she said.

"SHAKEN, AND STIRRED"

Vietnam in 1998 was not what I called a police state.

This was due to its economic reform policy. Only the Communist governments that were unreformed were dependent upon authoritarian means to stay in power. Thus, on each and every city block in Cuba and North Korea was a government spy for the internal police force.

I have never been a Commie hater. Nor an admirer.

Communists seemed to universally believe that the ends justified any means, including wholesale slaughter. But it was fair to say that, as a philosophy, Marxism originally seemed intent on making people more happy overall in response to the abuses of the Industrial Revolution.

Compared to, say, National Socialism.

Marx himself was no rube fanatic. As with Albert Einstein, he was an intellectual with a keen eye for irony. Marx wrote, *"Historical events enact themselves first as tragedy and then, in their repetition, as farce."*

It was my belief that both the Chinese and Vietnamese governments were, by 1998, in more ways similar, than dissimilar, to our contemporary American state. Was Captain America running out of reasons to hate the Commies, and vice versa? Perhaps.

I figured that governments were no longer the prime worry when it came to starting ruinous conflicts. The next world war, if it occurred in the near future, would more likely be religious.

Vietnam seemed to be one of the safest spots in the world for a tourist. Even police were unarmed. Excepting the rifle range at Cu Chi, I did not see guns the whole time. Although Saigon at first appeared somehow dangerous, I came to believe that my initial impression was mistaken.

On the Internet, travelers reported that it was a place where women could travel safely alone. Even sexual harassment was minimal.

If not a police state, Vietnam was authoritarian, as in control of the media. Outside Saigon it was hard to buy foreign newspapers, and the government after all, published the *Viet Nam News* that portrayed its benefactor as a well-intended, grandfatherly institution. The newspaper was usually interesting to read. I remembered a story with pictures about a tourism project to recreate a former guerilla base where, I assumed primarily Australians, could come play at war. Throwing hand-grenades, minus the detonators. Shooting fish with bows-and-arrows.

"Sai Gon army posts will be recreated over 1.4 hectares in the village which will also have houses that have not changed their appearance for nearly four decades.

Utilizing wasp hives, bamboo stakes, spears, and cross-bows did not deter the heroic people of Ben Tre Province in the Mekong Delta from joining the nation's 21-year struggle against the U.S. imperialists. The province plans to pay homage to its heroic people by re-creating scenes of the guerilla war waged against the U.S. and its puppet regime. The plan involves turning Dinh Thuy village into a tourist attraction."

Wasp hives, and bamboo stakes.

I'd say: Put the next one in Synney, mate.

After we returned to the U.S., I read an interview with a former Montagnard fighter in *Vietnam*, a magazine about the war. The Montagnard settled in San Francisco long ago, getting out on a boat and onto an American ship off Vung Tau, as Saigon fell in 1975. Most of the interview was about his experience at Lang Vei, a Special Forces camp overrun by tanks in 1968, marking the first use of armor by the North.

He "led an interesting life," as they put it in the old Chinese curse. After Lang Vei, he escaped into Laos and stayed with fellow tribesman for several years of contented, traditional village life. That was, until three escaped GIs from a prison camp in Vietnam showed up in the Laotian village one day and pleaded with him to guide them to safety in Vietnam.

The Montagnard was ready to go home, anyway, so he guided them through the jungle for a month, carrying spears and crossbows. They came upon a small VC camp, where the Americans knifed two VC and captured their AK-47s. The group made it safely to Kontum. The captain in the group gave him a letter of recommendation to American authorities, which later allowed him to board a Navy ship in 1975.

He hiked to his village only to find out that his father had been shot. South Vietnamese soldiers had raped his sister. The provincial chief had allowed this, and had confiscated rice paddies as well as forest land, and sold them to businessmen.

"The provincial chief lived in Quang Ngai, but he came to Gia Vuc for an inspection. I watched him and hid in a tree and killed him with one shot. My hate was over. The government soldiers looked for me, but they could not find me in the jungle.

If they caught me, they would punish all my people. So I left for Saigon. I never returned to my home. I could never see my family again. I was now alone."

With neither food nor money, he made it out. His sponsor was a pastor in Minnesota. The Montagnard liked Minnesota.

"I worked in a factory making clothes. I saved my money so I could go to the warm weather. The people in Minnesota are friendly, like my own people, but it was too cold for me.

Here in California I am among many Vietnamese, but some

think I am unworthy because I am from the mountains. There is something I will tell you."

I had met quite a few Vietnamese immigrants in the past, and had never considered the issue that this man was about to bring up:

"There are many Vietnamese Communists in America. They are both men and women spies. They watch over us. I am not afraid of them. They want to forget the war. The Vietnamese government wants American money and goods. They don't like us to talk about the war. Rich men give them money to live on. I am poor, but I am happy here.

They know us and they watch us. Some of my friends get letters from Vietnam. The young people in Vietnam don't know much about the war. They only know the Communists, and they want to go to the cities. They have forgotten the old ways."

This made me so curious that I was stirred to ask Petite's brother-in-law in Los Angeles about it.

He listened, as I explained the allegation about the spies in America.

Then he curled his lip, and said, "I wouldn't doubt it."

"HA LONG BAY"

I was not sure what to expect when we boarded a tourist van in rainy Hanoi but I was certain I would enjoy Ha Long Bay, having seen many beautiful pictures of this most famous of all Vietnamese natural wonders.

Petite had called Auntie who recommended a particular travel agent. The man had come to the hotel on Monday. It was only twenty dollars each for the round trip, one night's hotel, eight hours of boat tours. Meals for almost two days.

For some reason, I would have felt better if it had cost more. There was an old saying in Vietnam, "Someone always has to pay."

After a five-hour ride on a hard seat, the van rolled into Ha Long on an overcast day, passed through town, and headed up a steep hill. Perched on a cliff, the hotel providing a commanding view - especially from our fourth-story room. We put up our bags and walked downstairs to find the tables on the ground floor set up for lunch.

This was the part I was not looking forward to.

The group of ten on the tour gathered for lunch. I was not hungry, the result of belting down a huge American breakfast at the Eden, figuring the odds as to whether it would be the last edible food for two days until we returned to civilization.

Under dreary skies, the five-hour drive had again seemed like Korea, although the weather was the same as San Diego in June. Overcast, foggy. But here, bright green rice paddies and magically shaped limestone islands had presented themselves toward the end of the journey.

We pulled our white plastic chairs to a white plastic table.

Petite had always thought me picky, not an adventurous eater. But my native culture was not among those which gobbled up anything that moved and I was known to eat exotic fare on occasion, such as lobster, shrimp, mushrooms; even oysters on the half shell when red sauce, beer, and crackers were available.

"Picky" was a relative term at best.

Seated at the table, we introduced ourselves for the first time. Everyone had simply tried to nod off and endure the morning trip. There were two young nurses from Norway, a Chinese couple from Hainan who looked to be about my age. Two Frenchmen and a French girl in their early thirties from Paris. A 27-year-old Vietnamese female businesswoman.

Except for Petite, the Asian women were outfitted in high heels and dresses. The Chinese husband had on a leisure suit with a sweater. Everyone else was attired for a day at the beach.

Petite had chatted with the Vietnamese business lady in the van along the way. The businesswoman now announced that she would meet us at the dock in an hour. She hopped onto the back seat of a scooter driven by a handsome young man. They vanished down the hill.

Petite said, "Oh good. More for us!"

Everyone laughed, though the French had pretended not to speak English. It was obvious they understood everything we said. As with most French travelers in Vietnam they were wearing stupid looking hats. However, they seemed to favor wide-bodied Converse All-Star tennis shoes of various colors and I liked the maroon color: Skateboardy. X-Games. Dude.

Kids wore those at home. $19.95 at Cal Stores.

I had on a pair of swim trunks, flip-flops, and a white "Hook 'Em" tee shirt with a bull dorado pictured on the back about to chomp a herd of anchovy.

Petite had a sweater around her waist. She was in blue-jean shorts, flip-flops, and a tee shirt from Belize that read: "Bite Me."

An incongruous, international group, if ever there was one.

Petite explained, "This is a traditional Vietnamese meal!"

Indeed it was. Soup, followed by four different courses, now being hurried onto the table by the entire family who owned the hotel.

The food smelled fine.

Surprise! It was good, especially the spring rolls.

Next, we all hurried into the van and it pulled up at a public dock ten minutes later. Our group was the first onto a boat, which seated about forty in its cabin on nice leather cushions.

I explored the topside, accessing it by ladder. When I got back downstairs to our seat, another group of passengers was boarding. The Norwegian girls sat across the table from us, but there was room in our booth for two more people.

The boat was not completely full after the second group boarded. I figured that would be it. We stretched out a little.

One of the girls across from us wanted a coffee. She explained in perfect English that she was a caffeine addict.

I ordered a beer, then I asked the Norwegians: "*Ha Long* you been here?"

Pause.

They laughed.

The blond nurse told us she was planning a trip to Peru for next year. By herself, no less. The brown-haired nurse laughed a lot and drank coffee. That is, if you called *Nescafe* coffee.

I said, "I wouldn't let *my* daughter travel to Peru alone."

They laughed again.

I guessed that was the point.

"By the way, *Ha Long* you gonna be in Peru?"

It could have gone on forever. Mercifully a final group

boarded and another Norwegian girl, whom they both knew, took the place next to them.

I saw a six-foot-four fellow with thick glasses, dressed for a safari and bending over, making his way down the aisle under the low ceiling. He landed in the empty cushion next to me and took off his floppy, camouflage hat to reveal a baldpate.

He turned out to be a fellow American. Originally an East Coaster, who had graduated from U.C. Santa Cruz, he taught at a university in Japan. It was Spring Break. He would be on his way to Thailand after this.

His name was Jed. He was quite the *raconteur*. We hit it off immediately and talked for twenty minutes when I had to get up to use the rest room.

On the way out of the ship's head, I spotted our guide, Ngoc, who was in his twenties. I asked him when we would be getting under way.

He said, "Now." Pointing at the Vietnamese business lady being helped aboard, high heels and all, by two men.

We finally left port. It was a slow, pleasant boat ride on a calm bay.

Jed had been living in Japan for the past ten years, during which he had visited Vietnam several times. He had been "going slow this time," he said.

I told him how it was impossible for me to become an ex-patriot, unless I could get footie and baseball games on television. After I said it, I figured this would not be a problem for him. Although he was large, Jed's gentlemanly demeanor and lily-white skin suggested someone you might see hiking in Borneo netting butterflies.

But he did understand, after all. He said, "Oh, American ex-pats soon get into Sumo wrestling, Harry. Feed that Sports Bug!"

Now that was some factoid.

Sumo Wrestling. *Who would have thought?*

I asked about the quality of life in Japan for Japanese.

What he said about it was mostly as I had imagined it, except that Japanese students only killed themselves while studying in high school. Once they made to college, it was hard to flunk out. (Ivy League). Oh, and they liked to party.

The last part sounded somehow familiar.

The boat started to chug past mushroom-shaped islands.

Jed and I went on deck to take in the view. Over the rail was a partial fog, brightening suddenly at times with breaks in the cloud cover. Slowly the boat cruised in front of what looked like a fjord; a narrowing water valley, vertical green cliffs on each side fading into a far-away fog bank toward misty mountains.

Where the spirits flew, I supposed.

Next we passed another set of islands. These resembled small animals, rodent-like creatures. I stood on deck too long admiring one. It seemed alive.

Too late, I got the camera up and stared through the viewfinder.

Nada. The island was now covered by fog.

Huge limestone formations at ninety-degree angles materialized out of the mist ahead. It felt almost like being on a riverboat.

After thirty minutes, Jed and I went back in the cabin. We could see most of the scenery through the glass.

I said, "We hear that lifetime employment by Japanese companies is becoming a thing of the past."

Jed said, "Oh, not as much as you think. Once employed, it's pretty much for life unless you break the rules. It's still a big deal to fire someone... a very messy scene, Harry. Especially if the employee objects; then it's like a family fight."

We ordered more beer.

The three Norwegians and Petite came back inside.

For their benefit, I asked Jed loudly, "*Ha Long*... you been here?"

The Norwegians went into hysterics.

Petite could only shake her head. It was hopeless.

Jed was bewildered. "Almost a month," he said, thinking I meant: How long had he been in the country?

He mentioned that he got his wallet picked in Nha Trang.

I began a lecture on the subject of how to carry a wallet around without getting it picked. The instant Expert-On-Almost-Anything. Soon everyone at the table was about to nod off, when the brunette nurse piped up and said that people had warned her about carrying handbags in Hanoi at night. That kids rode around on motorbikes grabbing them.

Petite said that the nurse should have known women didn't carry purses at night anywhere, not realizing that in Norway amazingly enough, it was not a problem.

Jed announced that he *did* manage to get his wallet back.

"The guy who stole it," he said, "came up to me on the street the next day in Nha Trang. He wanted to sell it back. The wallet he took contained only some keys to my backpack. That's why I never bother guarding it. I've got an extra set in my pocket."

Touché.

He pulled the aforementioned keys out of his baggy pants pocket, as if to prove to the girls that he wasn't making this up.

"The Vietnamese wanted 30,000 for my wallet. I started to reach toward my pants like I was going to pay him, I grabbed my wallet with one hand and hit him in the face with the other. He fell down, then ran away... So I got back my wallet and extra keys."

I said, "You had more fun in Nha Trang than we did."

He told me that he had spent the past week in the Central Highlands.

"It's *interesting*," he said.

By now, I no longer figured he had traveled there to net butterflies. A quick age-check told me he was too young to have been in the war.

He said, "I'm interested in indigenous peoples."

This prompted the two Norwegians to tell us about their trip, which they booked at the *Green Bamboo* in Hanoi. It was a tour to see the mysterious Red Muong People for a day.

Petite chatted with them about it.

Jed said, "Anyway, the Central Highlands: Pleiku. Buon Me Thuot... I had an indigenous guide, a cute girl who spoke English. It's a lot poorer up there. She was picked out specifically from the Jarai people and sent to the coast for education. She was supposed to advocate the government view, you see, but all she talked about was how the government doesn't do enough for the people. It's the same everywhere."

It made me glad that we had not ventured to the hinterlands when he said that there was little jungle left in the highlands.

I asked, "Because of Agent Orange?"

He laughed. "I thought the same at first. So I quizzed the bus driver, who said it was still mostly jungle even after the war. The trees were cut down over the past ten years by government-sponsored logging companies."

I asked, "Wasn't there a lot of unexploded ordnance around in the Central Highlands?"

I had heard that there was, even at the Champa site of M y Son, a national park. *"Don't stray far from the towers, as un-exploded mines may still be in the ground,"* advised the guidebook.

Jed wrinkled his face in thought.

"Well, *I* never stepped on any," he said.

"RELIABLE CHINESE SAUCES"

I was the first awake as usual. It was another misty morning. The shower room was very basic with limited hot water and a scrimpy strand of cotton fiber to dry off with.

Yet it was a greedy thrill to be having so much fun for so little cash. The hotel may have looked like Pyongyang, but the chow was good and it seemed as if the whole trip to Ha Long was free. Something we might have found behind Door Number Three.

"Let's see what the Trumans have won, Monty!... Why it's a two-day trip to Ha Long Bay, courtesy of the kind folks who set the exchange rate for the U.S. Dollar."

What a deal.

"Give 'em a hand, Monty."

Petite was out of bed and taking a shower when I arrived downstairs. I was the first one there. Everything was closed. Shortly after 7 a.m. things got going. Food arrived at the table.

I ordered a *Nescafe,* grabbing a fresh baguette, butter and jam.

The Chinese couple appeared and the man sat next to me. He informed me that they had been on a walk since 6 a.m.

So he claimed the Early Bird award for the group.

His English was not bad at all. He was the general manager of a manufacturing company on Hainan island, the southernmost point in China, about 300 miles southeast of Ha Long Bay. Almost as large an island as Formosa, Hainan extended as far as south as Vinh; roughly the upper third of Vietnam. The body of water between Hainan and west to the coastline was the Gulf of Tonkin.

His name was Wong Kai.

I asked him how his wife was enjoying the tour.

"Oh!" he laughed vigorously. "She not *wife*."

Apparently, from what I could gather, she was a "business associate." It was a little hazy.

Wong Kai said, "First trip abroad!" and pointed at her proudly.

Smiling, gently nodding her head in my direction, she acknowledged that we were discussing her. She had no idea what we said.

In terms of distance, she was "abroad" no farther than, say, a day trip to Tijuana from Santa Barbara. Interesting use of terms. But if she thought she was abroad, she *was*, as far as I was concerned.

Petite came down the stairs and I introduced her to the Chinese couple.

Wong Kai said, "Call me W.K."

Before I could clue Petite, she asked W.K. how long he had been married.

"Ten years," he said, smiling, his pudgy fingers lifting a tea cup.

A family waitress came up to the table.

I ordered a fried egg that came free with breakfast. Again it tasted much better than the American variety. Why couldn't California hens put out eggs like that?

W.K. volunteered the information that his home, Hainan, was "much more beautiful than Vietnam." He encouraged us to visit. He had been to Vietnam twenty times; all on business.

I asked, "How do the Chinese feel about the Vietnamese?"

It was a loaded question this early in the morning. Petite was turned away, busily eating and talking to the Norwegian girls across the table.

W.K. said, "We don't feel anything particularly."

He explained that, in general, the Chinese did not pay a lot of attention to Vietnam because the country was so backward economic-wise that it was "irrelevant."

When I asked W.K. which countries *were* relevant, he recited the usual list of suspects: America, Europe, Japan.

The main problems he had encountered in Vietnam were bureaucracy and the lack of infrastructure, the same problems our company encountered in China in the 1980s. I had seen the infrastructure sprout up almost overnight around Shenzen, which bordered Hong Kong. I had seen it in the process of construction; roads, bridges, airports. Red dirt roads became freeways in less than a year. Skyscrapers popping up like pimples.

I told W.K. about it, then I asked how things were in China these days.

"Very good!" he said. The government was currently re-verting houses to private ownership, and the state bank was now issuing 20-year loans at 3% interest.

Not exactly what Marx had in mind.

I said, "A banking system based on real property seems to be evolving."

When he grinned enthusiastically, I took it to mean that he endorsed the private property reform above all others.

While we were in Vietnam, two articles about China appeared in the *International Herald Tribune.*

From **"China's Real Agents of Change? Just Plain Folks"** by Thomas L. Friedman:

"Xu Guilan is a 56-year-old schoolteacher from Heng Dao. In her village, like others, you find many successful peasant farmers' families living in three attached houses: The first is a

small mud-brick hovel where the family lived under Mao; the second is a larger, red brick structure, built under Deng Xiaoping, and the third is a white-brick home with painted tiles around the front door, built in the Jiang Zemin era.

'Because of Deng Xiaoping we are getting richer,' Mrs. Xu explained. 'Both my sons work in the town now, one in a bank, one as a teacher. The big change for my family is that we now have a color TV.'

There are millions of Xu Guilans in China today. As long as the economy soars, the government can get away with just liberalizing the economics and not politics. But sooner or later this economy will slow. There will be pain.

The Chinese stock markets are poorly regulated and casinolike. Unless the government installs some real regulatory systems, one day they are going to crash. The biggest urban riots in China in the past few years have been led by disgruntled stockholders.

Ultimately, you cannot have democracy without democrats. Where will they come from? One of the most striking things about China today is the ideological vacuum left by the death of communism. Some Chinese are trying to return to religion or superstition; others opt for the most crass, unrestrained materialism.

China has gone from Mao to Milken without ever stopping at Madison. That is going to be a problem."

From **"Here Comes An Unemployment Crisis For China"** by Edward Steinfeld:

"The irony of the Asian financial crisis is that China, seemingly least involved, is about to suffer the most monumental consequences.

The source of China's trouble lies in its ailing state

enterprises, which employ most of the nation's urban workers. Two decades ago, at the dawn of reform, Chinese leaders committed themselves to keeping state firms afloat in order to maintain full urban employment. That commitment has necessitated massive infusions of capital.

To put it simply, the Chinese banking system is currently insolvent.

Policymakers are caught in a nasty predicament. Doing nothing and allowing a continuation of state-sector bailouts raises the specter of a total banking collapse. Indeed, policymakers already fear that with all the news of East Asian trouble rolling in, Chinese depositors will remove their savings from the banks and thus lay bare the insolvency of the system.

Yet undertaking the measures needed to preserve the financial system almost guarantees massive unemployment and social dislocation in China's cities."

Revolutionary situations often occurred at times when the rush of expectations met the reality of diminishing returns. For that reason, I believed that Vietnam would continue to have a Communist government much longer than China would.

The Vietnamese were still relatively poor. Their hopes for a better life in the future seemed more of a wish than an expectation.

And Vietnam seemed more aware than China of the inherent threat that prosperity would bring to its own existence.

"EVERYONE"

On the boat again. The morning tour. We drifted into a pristine emerald lagoon, everyone silently drinking in the view. Only an occasional sound. A camera shutter going off. A bird in the distance started to flap its wings, rippling the quiet bay.

Almost religious was the timeless mood, until a cellular telephone began ringing somewhere in the cabin.

Frantically the Vietnamese business lady yanked it from her purse. She started screaming at a supplier for her water pump factory; the irate customer having a tissy over the phone about some parts that didn't get to the factory on time.

Most of us Westerners on the boat did not fail to shoot her a dirty look or two.

Out of the magic lagoon and on the way to the next sight, the boat chugged along at a healthy pace. I was chatting on deck with Jed regarding his time with the Montagnard, when I saw a sampan racing faster than our vessel start to pull onto what looked like a colliding course. It swooped alongside, and we saw a rope come from over the rail.

Jed and I glanced at each other. Both boats were still moving.

We went over to where the sampan people were tying on. They were not pirates, but a floating shell shop with a large display of broken crustaceans and bleached coral.

The three Parisians ran up and peeked over the side, cursing the sampan people in French. *Les Species En-Daingered*, or something to that effect. The young woman shouted, *"L'Ecologie!"*

Most of us were less than mildly interested in what was for sale. Turning away, one of the Norwegians commented, "It's best not to buy anything. It only encourages them to strip the reef."

Granted it was already dead when they picked it up, but I wouldn't lug around a half-ton of bleached coral under any circumstances. I agreed.

The sampan remained strapped to the side of our boat for awhile. They had sold nothing. The Vietnamese business lady, now alone inside the cabin, got off the phone. She wandered onto the deck oblivious to the ruffled looks. Then, seeing the sampan people, she shrieked for joy.

She bought enough white coral to fill two plastic grocery bags.

Once she did this, all three Frogs went into an utter tizzy, barely composing themselves even after the sampan sped away.

The Vietnamese business lady could have cared less. She came by and merrily chatted with Petite.

Petite agreed with her that it was easy to save the world on a full stomach.

I got up and moved away cautiously, lest the others onboard think that I was on their side.

Back toward the engine room, I saw our guide, Ngoc.

Standing and reading a book, he looked up and said hello.

I stopped to chat, and told him that the tour was really neat, and asked him where we were headed next.

He said, "We're on the way to Dying Virgin Cave, where we'll get off the boat and walk through. That's the farthest point. Then the boat will head back, but we'll stop at a place where you can rent a local ferry to visit a grotto which was in the movie, *Indochine*."

I had seen the movie a long time ago. A boring film. I didn't remember much else about it, except that Catherine Denevieux was in it.

I asked Ngoc, "Has anyone ever counted all the islands in Ha Long Bay?"

"Around 1,600 of them, I think."

I told him, "You speak English very well."

"Thank you," he said. "I graduated from law school a couple of years ago, but wasn't able to find a job in the field of law. Besides, tour-guide pays better."

Certainly had a legal mind, I figured.

"I'm trying to get into business school now," Ngoc said.

I asked, "When you were a schoolboy did you ever hear of the My Lai massacre?"

"My Lai," he said. "You mean, in history? Yes."

Then a pregnant pause.

"Okay. Did you ever hear anything about the Hue Massacre during Tet in 1968?"

He shook his head. "We don't study such things," he said.

I had an old friend in Hanoi, actually the *original* Reliable Sauce, who worked for the government, and I trusted him for a reason. He reminded me of Petite. He had the same capacity for directness that she often displayed. A Vietnamese way of cutting through to the issue; at times at the expense of what Western society considered "courtesy."

Briefly, *Too* honest.

Vietnam was no Emily Post world.

I had met with Reliable Sauce at *Pho 66*, a soup stand off a busy Hanoi sidewalk, during which I had asked him the same question I asked Ngoc.

Reliable Sauce stopped slurping soup.

"Surely, the history of Vietnam has been somehow rewritten. It's really ugly," he said. "As far as the Hue massacre by the

VC, I was only aware of it myself not long ago. So I guess the northern people don't know."

Reliable Sauce stared into his soup bowl like it was a divining pool. He said, "The Tet Offensive was a terrible mistake, as far as military strategy. So after the war it was renamed."

"Renamed what?"

"*The Training-Step for the 1975 Offensive.*"

"Clever!" I noted.

Appreciatively, he smiled. It quickly faded.

He said, "Tet did make the U.S. negotiate to end the war. But all information was closed about how many soldiers were killed and how the VC army was destroyed after the battle."

I had time to clear up one more matter.

"I don't get it," I confessed. "Why did they ever let Bao Ninh publish **The Sorrow of War** here in Vietnam?"

He looked around casually.

"At first, many publishers refused it. Fear of trouble with the government. But the publisher of the Vietnamese Writers Association finally printed it under the title, **The Fate of Love**. There was a debate all over the hierarchy: What to do about this? Fortunately at the time the supporting people won. I was one of those," Reliable Sauce said. "There are periods when our government has a mild approach to literature. I think it was the first novel to point out certain situations: That nobody was happy after the war. That all soldiers suffered syndromes from it."

Reliable Sauce suddenly put his spoon aside, now looking for his raincoat.

"And everyone... Everyone was wicked in the fighting."

The water color in Ha Long Bay was unique. It was green, tempered with white limestone sediments. The visibility looked to be about ten feet. The sediments made it look slightly milky but clean, and the ocean was calm. It reminded me of fresh-water limestone pools in the Yucatan.

The water temperature was cold this time of year, about 60 degrees. Almost everyone I talked to on the boat said that they wished it were Summer now, so they could jump in. It was inviting because it didn't *look* cold.

The boat pulled up to the beach on an island. A crew-member tossed a wood two-by-four onto the sand and propped it against the vessel. Our gangplank. Somehow, no one, even in high heels, was killed, incapacitated, or injured on the way down.

Forty of us soon gathered in a cove in front of the opening to a massive cave.

Ngoc got up to give his first speech of the trip. In English, of course. First he asked if there were any Chinese in the audience.

W.K. timidly raised a hand.

Ngoc said, "So sorry... But it was near here in 938 AD on the Bach Dang river that General Ngo Quyen lured the Chinese navy upriver at high tide. His men had planted metal stakes in the riverbed. When the Vietnamese counterattacked at low tide, the invaders were driven into the stakes and were destroyed. This battle ended 1,000 years of Chinese rule."

Ngoc graciously smiled in W.K.'s direction.

In a booming stage voice, W.K. announced, "China forgives you!"

The audience roared.

Ngoc told a story about why it was named the Dying Virgin Cave, which I failed to remember. Then he directed the group to form one line to tour the cavern.

Petite and I had been casually holding hands, when she disappeared like a shot.

As the dust settled, Petite was second in line behind the Vietnamese business lady.

Petite yelled back, "Come on up here, Harry!"

The others turned, staring at me.

I shook my head because I headed naturally to the rear of any line. There I found Jed waiting.

Petite disappeared as we started moving and she entered the cave. They always said that opposites attract.

At the back of the line, Jed and I were able to take our time. There was no one behind us. It was darkish. There were stalactites and stalagmites. Finally, another passageway, and an opening into a stunning natural amphitheater. As sunlight beamed through the immense opening high above, I saw blue sky.

Everyone seemed fixated upon this hole in the roof, as if it were something we all had seen as cave men.

The outline of Jed's baggy safari outfit made it all seem like an *Indiana Jones* episode. Or better still, as if I had been traipsing, like a bothersome blue-tail fly, behind Catherwood and Stephens in the Maya Yucatan of the mid-Nineteenth Century.

Ha Long Bay changed colors here and there as we slowly motored back. Milk-green in more shallow waters. Turquoise in the deeper areas.

A few of the islands harbored a number of sampans and we saw ship traffic at one point, but most of the islands or outcroppings were deserted and sublime.

One that was not was the island with the famous grotto.

After we anchored, the boat was surrounded by five little barge-shaped wooden vessels that looked as if they had been patched together out of shingles. One ferry held a pair of industrious ten-year-old girls, each with a dilapidated paddle in hand.

Petite wisely boarded a bigger one with eight other people.

The little girls had four passengers, at a fare of 20,000 dong per head.

Only a few of us stayed behind. For awhile I talked to an Australian woman in her fifties on the fore deck. She had traveled extensively. She was by herself on this tour, but the Scandinavian kids kept her company, she said.

Up on the rooftop, I chatted with a Danish gal in her twenties; attractive, with sun-bleached hair and a dark tan. She was going all the way around the world on a two-year trip. She had come to Vietnam via India, Burma, Thailand, and Cambodia.

I snapped a few pictures and read my book.

Petite's ferry returned, and others began filtering back. She said the grotto was okay. She liked the little ferry trip better than the grotto.

Jed told me I should have gone.

But I was sure I could find some post cards, if I wanted to, and after Petite's assessment I felt I hadn't missed much. The place had not left an indelible impression from the movie. I went outside to smoke a cigarette.

The Australian woman was still on the fore deck. We were shooting the breeze, when Ngoc came out and announced that the captain was pulling anchor and taking off.

As soon as he said it, a foghorn blew twice.

The boat engines started up. I heard the anchor motor grind.

"Stop!" the Australian yelled. "Bloody Stop!"

Two of her new Danish friends were not back aboard from the grotto trip. She scurried inside and located Ngoc.

He explained it to the captain, who sent the anchor down once more. Still, the missing boat was nowhere in sight and it was getting towards twilight. The captain called to a passing sampan. He got them to look for the missing passengers.

After ten minutes or so, a sampan appeared out of the fog, towing the ferry captained by the tiny ten-year-olds. The tide had been running in. They had had no problem getting to the grotto, but they couldn't row the ferry back.

The Aussie lady had saved four fellow passengers at least a considerable inconvenience.

We had still another free meal coming at the hotel before we left on the bus to go back to Hanoi.

The Vietnamese business lady leaned and whispered something to Ngoc. Again she took off on a motorbike with her associate.

This seemed to relax the French contingent. Petite and I had a nice chat with them in English during lunch. They were young working folks living in Paris, which seemed to make Petite envious.

"Tough life," she kidded them.

"Oh, yes," the French girl said solemnly.

It was excellent food again. Soon almost everyone was aboard the bus at one o'clock.

By 1:20, we had been sitting long enough without moving that questions were being raised. Ngoc told us we would be leaving in exactly ten minutes. I decided to get off until the driver got on. The Parisians demanded that we leave behind the Vietnamese business lady, the only one not accounted for.

This delay did not seem to bother either the driver, or Ngoc, or Petite.

At 1:31 p.m. I stomped out a cigarette and told Ngoc, "Leave the damn bitch here!"

Five minutes later, she finally rode up and jumped off the motorbike with, what else? A big grin. She missed the silent treatment from the back of the bus because she took off her shoes and caught a nap.

On the ride back to Hanoi the weather was much clearer than it had been the day before. We passed a coal mining town with black streets. Green rice fields stretched to the horizon for the much of the trip.

Along the way, Petite pointed out a sign as we sped past.

"Dog For Sale," it said in Vietnamese.

As in: To Eat.

This was an infamous area of Vietnam that had a prodigious rat problem in the fields. Cat, like dog, was considered a culinary treat. The government had responded by forbidding consumption of felines, together with drastic penalties, and by putting a 1,000-dong reward on each rodent tail brought in by local "bounty hunters."

I turned to my wife, and said, "*Mon Petite*, if you're nice to me, I'll get you a job counting rat-tails."

She declined.

I resumed my gaze out the window, wondering where one might apply for a job such as that.

"PERSPECTIVE"

Petite grew up in Vietnam from 1946-1967, and returned for visits in 1970, 1972, 1991, 1993, as well our trip in 1998. She witnessed immense change.

I casually interviewed her one Sunday afternoon around the swimming pool. At first, she didn't want to talk.

She said, "You don't want to write about me, my life was boring. The war never affected me. I was in the city. I hardly knew it was going on."

Typical. I'd have to beat it out of her.

Petite was a great prosecutor yet a reluctant witness. She was very much American, but retained many Vietnamese vestiges. As with everyone in the world, eating habits were formed early and lasted a lifetime. She would prefer to eat her native food every day if it were available. And to this day she covered her food with hot sauce so that everything, even charcoal-broiled steak, ended up tasting somehow Asian.

Another vestige she retained was the belief that if a person had long ears this indicated a long life. Otherwise, with short ears. She seemed to be leery of dead bodies. She had managed to avoid seeing any first hand, so far. But other than normal gambling peccadilloes, she was not superstitious at all for a Vietnamese.

She did not have faith in organized religion, and seemed to believe that life was a punishment of some sort. I was, according to her, a manifestation of the hypothesis that she had clearly gone astray in a previous existence.

I asked her, "What has changed the most about Vietnam over the years?"

It took awhile but I knew she was formulating an answer, pacing the shallow end of the pool. The result of her deliberations was surprising in more ways than one.

Petite said, "Nowadays there is much more foreign influence than there was during the American times." It proved that perspective was everything. The current version of history, both American and Communist, seemed to portray otherwise: That the South Vietnamese were puppets to American overlords.

To say that foreign influence was more pervasive now than in the past was simply another way of saying that the Global Village had arrived in Vietnam.

Common use of credit cards was unheard of until the 1990s. Now there were cell phones, worldwide long-distance connections, e-mail, the Internet, cable television, CNN and Star TV.

Pizza. Tex-Mex. Punk music, albeit without punks.

Tourists.

Jobs for the young, which never existed except in rice paddies. People showing up for appointments on time. International corporations manufacturing goods. Skyscrapers over downtown Saigon.

"So many things changed," she said, "and I think mostly for the better."

Petite added a contrary item to her list of changes: "But now they use dollars everywhere." She gave me a hard look. "I think you should have to use Vietnamese money in Vietnam."

To me, it seemed smart policy for the government to let the market determine the local currency rate; therefore eliminating the black market and allowing dollars to legally flow into state banks instead of offshore.

To Petite, the universal acceptance of dollars in even the smallest restaurants and shops seemed an invasion of sovereignty. And maybe it was, maybe it wasn't. In San Diego, not one cashier had ever told me that he preferred Deutchmarks to dollars when I bought a pint of ice cream at 7-Eleven. It would take getting used to if that were to happen.

I asked Petite, "What would you most like to see change in the future for Vietnam?"

This did not take long. "One thing which hasn't changed is that the young people still think anything foreign is better than anything Vietnamese. From a candy bar to a college education. That's ridiculous, it isn't like that at all, but they don't realize it. Some things are better in one society and worse in the other," she said. "And of course I hope to see a more prosperous country, a higher standard of living. But there are cultural obstacles to overcome that go beyond economics. Many Vietnamese don't trust banks, or even cash, for important transactions. When we sold Mother's house in Saigon a couple of years ago, the buyer paid in gold bars."

"What about banks?" I asked.

"Many Asians like to be able to touch their money so they keep it in the home, perhaps uncomfortable having to trust a bank."

"So almost all large private transactions are in gold?"

"They feel that paper money fluctuates too much in value."

Once again, perspective was everything.

"BAC HO"

Friday was our last full day in Vietnam. A light, warm rain fell; it was never sunny in the North or stormy in the South while we were there.

We discovered that the Ho Chi Minh Mausoleum was closed again today but it would be open tomorrow morning from 8 to 11. Our flight would not leave until late the next afternoon, so we decided to come back to see Ho's corporal remains on Saturday.

On the same grounds, the Ho Chi Minh Museum was open, however. I expected little from the museum, figuring it would be another propaganda barrage.

The ground floor was mainly restaurants, shops, and meeting rooms. The second floor also had little to do with Ho. It was a compendium of recent Party history, as well as economic advances, which included the porcelain toilet bowl exhibit, the display for Vietnam Airlines, and photos of various ethnic groups hobnobbing with visiting bigwigs.

A sweeping set of stairs led up to an atrium dominated by twelve-foot bronze statue of the man born as Nguyen Sinh Cung in 1890, known to the world as Ho Chi Minh.

From here, two sets of short steps led in either direction to the museum itself. We chose the right side and came upon a "field" of polished bronze water lilies on a marble floor with a straw hutch beside it, representing Ho's birthplace in Hoang Tru.

From this point the exhibits were laid out in a circle above the atrium, continuing clockwise chronologically according to Ho's life. It was the finest looking museum I had seen outside of Paris.

We next encountered an enclosed section with many mirrors

and small passageways, the mirrors reflecting off each other. Displayed were photographs, artwork, and remembrances from early twentieth-century Paris, where Ho had lived for a number of years; emigrating to Marseilles as a galley boy aboard a passenger ship in 1911. In 1919, he had put on a diplomatic topcoat and tie in the capital city and presented President Woodrow Wilson with a list of grievances concerning the French occupation of Vietnam.

He was ignored.

He joined the French Communist Party and later explained: "It was patriotism, not communism, that inspired me."

In Hong Kong he formed the Indochinese Communist Party in 1929. Ho was soon arrested and thrown into prison.

The most startling item in the museum was a photo taken in 1938, just after he was released. It pictured a man in coat and tie with a lean handsome face and shaved head. Penetrating eyes. He looked so much like a modern day prizefighter that it reminded me of a young Marvin Hagler. Ho Chi Minh was 48 years old at the time. Americans were used to seeing him as an old man with a white goatee, but he remained youthful in appearance until his fifties.

The famous elderly visage and white goatee began to appear in the 1940s, perhaps due to the rigors of waging a guerilla war against the Japanese who invaded Vietnam in 1940. He had moved back to the country to form the Viet Minh, an acronym for the Vietnamese Independence League, and at this time adopted his final *nom de guerre*: Ho Chi Minh, "Bringer of Light."

There has been much discussion about Ho's true intentions at the end of World War II. He seemed to admire the principles of western democracies, if not the actual conduct, and he penned several pleas to President Roosevelt to establish an independent Vietnam. With his history as a leading Communist, as well as the American preoccupation at the time of saving French colonies and reestablishing the old political order, he was again ignored. We will probably never know whether an opportunity was missed, or if it was just a ploy.

Most of the exhibits in the museum dealt with the French colonial period. The Americans were hardly mentioned, as opposed to the museums in the South where it was vice-versa. I noticed that most of the younger Vietnamese skirted through the place, seldom reading the explanatory notes, whereas many of the older visitors studied them carefully.

For his entire life, Bac Ho was underestimated by his enemies. In a similar manner, I suppose, I had underestimated this tribute to his life before I had seen it. The museum took years to build. People from many nations, including France and Russia, had helped with its design. It was certainly a beautiful monument to one of the great figures in world history.

Bac Ho was first and foremost a nationalist. It was true that he became directly or indirectly responsible for an enormous degree of bloodshed. He was a product of the age of Lenin, raised in a colonial society. Each time he tried to reach out for an alternative to communism, he was denied. Finally, his goal of unification took such precedent for him that the means came to justify the ends.

An early believer in liberty and equality, it seemed that he adopted the communist methodology originally as a proven way to achieve a political end. It worked. He then refined the methodology to include the principles of guerilla warfare. In other words, at first he was *using* communism to achieve independence.

However, by the end of Ho's life and beyond, the false promise of the communist state was using him.

Petite and I took a taxi back to the hotel for lunch. We divided one four-cheese pizza, a spinach salad, and an apple pie a-la-mode.

A middle-aged lady came to the table and introduced herself as the manager of the restaurant. She looked like a veritable "grande dame" of the opera, with a black dress and too much makeup.

First she thanked us for dining at the restaurant so much, and then inquired about the meal, which was excellent. She told us she had formerly owned the Roxy Night Club in Hanoi.

"T'was *the* place to be, I assure you!" she said.

I couldn't tell by her accent, so I asked where she was from.

In a throaty voice, she said, "I came to Hanoi from Melbourne, Australia, three years ago on vacation. Visited a good friend. Absolutely fell in love with the place and decided to throw caution to the wind. I've lived here ever since."

I asked her how the business was doing.

There were only two other tables filled, both with French businessmen dressed impeccably in linen suits.

"God, it's awful. The restaurant is struggling. All because of the crisis," she said, referring to the Asian economic downturn which had started the previous summer in Thailand and Indonesia and had now spread to Japan and Korea, even threatening to become a world wide recession. "Companies simply stopped spending money overnight, last Fall."

Wistfully she looked around the room. "It used to be so crowded. This was the first place in Hanoi to offer Western food when it opened five years ago. The owner is a young man, I should say he's in his late twenties, with a Vietnamese father and Italian mother. Quite a gamble in those days. You couldn't even buy cheese, to speak of. Now there's a distributor in Saigon with sales agents here. The ingredients are all imported but no more trouble to get, really, than ordering for a place in Melbourne. Everything is available. At a price."

She glanced away toward the entrance, as if expecting

someone.

I told her I thought the Corona beer was a nice touch.

"Ah, yeh. The Aussies drink it."

"What happened with the Roxy?" I asked.

Her faced turned a bit melancholy. "It burned to the ground last November," she said. "I lost $500,000."

I didn't ask for details but surprisingly she said she knew who was responsible.

As a former restaurant owner, I found myself giving her a little wink before I knew it.

She said, "Around here there's no such thing as fire insurance for small businesses, my dear."

I asked her if the nightclub had served mostly foreign clientele.

Eyes now bright, she said, "Oh no! It was *perfect*. One-third Vietnamese. One-third ex-pat. One-third tourists. A fantastic spot. Have you seen the Roxy tee shirts around town? They're collectors items now."

I had seen not a one, but I had plenty of "collectors items" from my own places that had gone belly-up when the tourists went home, or when the Market crashed, or when we simply got tired of the hassles and threw in the bar towel.

She glanced at her watch.

"It's taken almost three months to get the paperwork ready for approvals for the new club," she told us. "I'm waiting for a man from the Ministry. He's supposed to meet at 2:00 to go over it all before we submit the application. Guess what? The bloody government's *my new partner*!"

"Really?" Petite asked.

Gee I wonder who set the fire? I thought.

"If you had told me three years ago when I was in Melbourne that I would now be living in Hanoi, Vietnam. Going into business with the Communist Party. Well..."

She left it unsaid.

Life!

"The bureaucracy is incredible here, especially since the bar business is considered a 'Social Evil.'"

"Is *Pizza* a Social Evil, as well?"

She gave a hearty laugh, slapping my back.

I supposed aloud, "The bar business ain't so evil, as long as the powers that be get a decent cut of the action."

After lunch we walked two blocks and managed to find the entrance to Hoa Lo prison, known in America but not in Vietnam as the "Hanoi Hilton."

It was located in a section of town named Hoa Lo, which Petite translated, "huge oven," such as used in ceramics. The neighborhood had been one where ceramics were manufactured.

The words also connoted "inferno," or "hell." This was apropos because Hollywood had yet to design a movie set as evil and dark as this place was. It made the Turkish jail in *Midnight Express* look like a day camp on Lake Winnemaca for Explorer Scouts.

The French built Hoa Lo Prison in 1896. Most of the original structures had been demolished to make way for the skyscraper next door. A portion was left standing and opened to the public because Hoa Lo Prison retained a significant role in Communist lore. During the French regime it was a prison solely for political people who opposed colonial rule: Nationalists, Communists, and such.

The current General Secretary of the Communist Party, Do Muoi, escaped from there in 1945. Hoa Lo Prison had other distinguished alumnae, including many in the aging leadership of today's regime, as well as Richard Peterson, the current U.S. Ambassador. Although the facility housed American POW pilots from 1964-1972, only a small plaque in a faraway corner mentioned this fact. What remained of the prison was a showcase to glorify revolutionary heroes.

A man at the entrance charged me 10,000 dong.

Just to make sure, Petite asked him, "I get in free, don't I?"

Even at the front gate the place looked forbidding enough that apparently she wasn't taking chances.

In what I interpreted as a example of the pervasive cynical mood, the man said, "Well, it's free now. But they will be charging Vietnamese starting next month!" Shaking his head with a sneer, as if to say, "Isn't that typical?" or "What will they think of next?"

Along the way, Petite stayed busy translating the explanatory signs throughout, as they were solely in Vietnamese, including the plaque about the American pilots.

The only other people we saw were a German group, who had brought their own guide and translator.

There were torture chambers, execution areas, many different types of cells, leg irons, a guillotine, even a "death row."

Thick black paint covered the torture chamber area, making it seem even more forbidding. We happened to be there at the same time the German group wandered through.

While peeking through a set of crooked bars at a garroting instrument, I suddenly heard, "MEIN GOTT!" directly behind me.

I wheeled around.

One of the Germans had rested his hand against the wall. When he removed it, his inner palm was black, slimed with fresh paint. Abnormally upset about it, he looked around frantically for a place to wipe it off. It seemed that everyone in the room sympathized completely. Not even his friends were joking about it. No Teutonic *Schadenfreude* today, thanks.

I didn't want any torture-chamber black on me, either.

In an open-air walkway nearby were several sculptured murals depicting life in prison: Chain gangs with manacles, beatings, a French guard pushing down an inmate's head into a trash can full of water. Nothing about it was the invention of propaganda. It had all happened, and here, and for over a half-century.

We went up the stairs to a small museum on the second story. A library contained picture albums filled with biographies of prisoners. I looked over a few of these for awhile until one exhibit in a glass case caught my eye.

It was a faded pinkish blanket, once red. On it was a crude, roundish yellow star of paper. This was the homemade "flag" raised above Hoa Lo Prison by its inmates in 1954 when the French were booted out.

For whatever reason, the almost child-like banner plucked an emotion. The scraggly blanket and paper star properly reflected the almost unimaginable poverty and grinding hardships that the inmates endured. I thought it sad they did not have a nice flag for their long awaited freedom from incarceration and victory celebration.

Back at the hotel, I headed upstairs to the room while Petite stayed below and chatted with the younger of the two doormen.

I tuned the television to CNN, which was reviewing the week's top story: Two high school students had ambushed class-mates at their high school in Jonesboro, Arkansas, killing four of them as well as a teacher. With guns so available in the United States, the incident neither particularly surprised nor shocked me.

Thirty minutes later, Petite burst through the door excitedly, explaining how the doorman had just spent the past twenty minutes loudly flaming all over the Communists, delivering a public harangue on the sidewalk right in front of the hotel.

First, he was bitter about the government dumping on the families of the soldiers who fought the war, now that it no longer had use for them. He told Petite of several old ladies who had lost every one of their children fighting in the South, and the government would not support them whatsoever.

I asked Petite if she knew how old the bellman was.

She said, "He's 35. He was a kid when the war ended. He's been in the Army, though. He hates officers and politicians."

"Who wouldn't?"

"The bellman told me he would line 'em all up and shoot them if he could."

After that, he started shouting about no free education, pointing to a grade school next door to the hotel. He said it cost 500,000 dong per year. Who could afford that? He complained that the Party bosses were getting rich and the poor were suffering. The elite's children got into the best schools; his own kids had no chance.

Petite said she thought the man was having a nervous breakdown when he walked to a parked bicycle nearby.

The bellman kicked the hell out of it and sent it sprawling.

"See! Vietnamese products are shit!" he screamed. "Copies! Nothing original. Can't even make a fucking bicycle. They fall apart after you buy one."

After he calmed a bit, Petite asked him, "Aren't you afraid to be shouting this in public?"

He pulled together his ruffled uniform and said, "No! I'm so disgusted with them, I don't even care."

After listening to the unexpected tale, I wondered if we would ever see the guy again.

Two middle-aged men in pith helmets, fatigue jackets and sandals, had spent the better part of each day crouched across the street. I had assumed they were informers of some sort, watching the Hotel Eden.

Would our doorman end up as a "guest" at a present day version of the "Hanoi Hilton?"

"HISTORY DOESN'T MATTER"

Our last night in Vietnam, we were to have dinner with Auntie Giang and family, at our invitation. Giang had chosen *Thuy Ta* restaurant overlooking Hoan Kiem Lake.

We were to meet at six p.m.

Petite and I traipsed down the hotel stairs, headed first for *Green Bamboo Cafe* to check it out because it was so famous with the backpack set. Many of them, including the Norwegian girls, had booked their tours there.

The young doorman merrily greeted Petite. He swung it open for us with a flourish.

I said, "*Cam On*" - noting that he had not been hauled away; at least not yet.

After a ten-minute stroll, we had no trouble finding what we were looking for. It began to sprinkle just as we ducked into the *Green Bamboo*.

At ten past five p.m. the place had two other customers, an Aussie fellow at the next table chatting with a French girl. They were doing beers. A soccer match on television garnered the attention of most of the Vietnamese employees. We ordered coffees and got up to look around.

In the back room was a paperback book exchange, without much inventory. Upstairs, a bar that looked cramped even when empty.

Back down the steps, our coffees sat on the dining table. At a desk on the opposite side of the room, a forlorn travel agent doodled his fingers. Various signs on the wall touted tours to the far North where one could eyeball, for a day, indigenous peoples:

246

Black Hmong, Red Hmong, Black Thai, White Thai, the Muong, the Nung, the Dao, or the Giay. One of the touted tours was to a village named Son La.

It rang a bell.

I recalled a naive notion I had before we left for the journey. A brother-in-law of Petite's had been a Colonel in the ARVN. He had spent five years after the war in several re-education camps, all of them in the far North. He had been transferred to four different sites between 1975 and 1980. First he was sent to Lao Cai on the China border, then to Yen Bai, then to Tuyen Quang, finally to a camp near Son La.

Before we left San Diego, I had considered hiring a driver to try to visit at least one of these. Petite's brother-in-law told me in 1981, shortly after arriving at our house in San Diego, that he had explained to an American consulate officer in Bangkok, during a relocation interview, that he had once seen a group of American POWs being led away from the camp by NVA guards.

He said that the American interviewer did not seem surprised, and had posed but a few follow-up questions. I asked the brother-in-law where he had seen them, and when. He said it was at the worst camp, Tuyen Quang. Probably in 1978. But he had lost track of time in the camps and could not be sure what year it was. At any rate, he had gotten the impression that the interviewer did not believe him. He swore to me that it was true, he didn't care whether anyone believed it or not. That's what he saw.

Whatever the truth, the *Green Bamboo* would not include guided tours to those places. Petite and I finished our coffees.

We headed out along the lakeside toward *Thuy Ta*.

Parked outside the restaurant on two Honda motorbikes we met Auntie Giang, her son Khai, daughter Tu, and son-in-law Huy.

Khai said that there was a lengthy waiting list inside, so we agreed to a nearby restaurant. Petite and I followed Tu and Huy as they walked their Honda for two short blocks.

Seated at the second restaurant, Auntie told us that Uncle Ky was not feeling well, and was sorry that he could not attend.

I sat next to Khai at dinner. I had been looking forward to meeting the younger members of the family and talking to children of the privileged class in Vietnam. All of them were dressed nicely; the young men in sport coats, slacks, and turtleneck sweaters. I felt unusually grubby in my dacron Bali shirt that reeked of deodorant, and rumpled jeans; both of which had been wadded in a suitcase for three weeks.

Huy and Tu were white-collar professionals in their late twenties. He was a structural engineer for a dam project, she a local controller for a Euro food conglomerate.

Khai, Giang's son, was 32 years old. He had just returned from a CAD-CAM computer design conference in Singapore.

First I went through the litany of questions that I asked of everyone.

Khai told me that he believed that most of the people in his circle of friends knew that both sides during the War of Liberation had committed atrocities. As to Hue, specifically, he had only been aware of it the previous week. While he was in Singapore, CNN had run a story about the massacre that he had happened to see.

As usual, when I mentioned to him that we stopped by the My Lai memorial, it only seemed to embarrass; provoking uneasy silence. Impolite to comment, I supposed.

As to the issue of why the government allowed **The Sorrow of War** to be published in Vietnam, he said, "Well, the book was first published abroad. People made copies of it. It became so popular, they *had* to allow it. Everybody was reading it, anyway."

I said, "I assume you read it."

"Oh yes. And I liked it. But a lot of people still don't."

At this time, brother-in-law Huy had appeared to be catching wisps of conversation. He was stiff, seemingly uncomfortable at this "family reunion" dinner. I was sure he didn't want to be here. It was obligatory.

Finally Huy leaned over tentatively and asked, "In your book about Vietnam, Harold, are you going to start with the North or the South first?"

I hardly ever discussed writing.

"I suppose Saigon first. Because it's where we arrived."

This produced drawn looks from both Huy and Khai.

It was my turn to be embarrassed, touched by the fact they would even care.

While the waitress served hors d'ouerves, I asked Tu and Huy if they had ever traveled out of Vietnam before.

Daughter Tu answered, "We attended a youth conference one summer in Germany when we were high school sweethearts," referring to her husband. "It was in Magdeburg, in the former East Germany."

I told them about my Army years listening to Communist functionaries in Magdeburg, recording their conversations from atop Teufelsberg Mountain in Berlin. Spying on them, in other words. I filled them in on how GIs didn't care much for the Prussians. Rambling on, this and that.

Tu mentioned that she had returned home at the end of that summer, but that Huy had stayed on to go to school.

"Did you like the Germans?" I asked Huy, assuming that he probably did not.

He said, "Yes. They are very nice people. All people are the same underneath the skin."

Harry The-American-Creep-Who-Hated-Everybody asked, "Well, what did you think of the German culture? After all, they're quite a bit different than the Vietnamese."

Huy paused to make sure I got the message.

He said, "I was only in Germany for a year, Harold. Not long enough to get to know anyone's culture in anything but a superficial manner."

Oooooooooooooooooooooooooh. **Gotcha**!

Mr. Know It All started backtracking: Explaining, much to Huy's delight, how people in America were still interested in Vietnam, how the book was simply about *impressions* during a three-week trip. How those impressions could be right. Or wrong. How the book might reflect as much about Americans as it did about the Vietnamese.

And so forth and so on.

The food arrived at the table. It was expensive and unappetizing. As I had done so often in China under similar circumstances, I chose the option of orally injecting the many nutrients in Heinekens while watching others eat. At the end of the meal, the waitress rolled out bowls of fresh tropical fruit. Despite Petite's entreaties, I refused the mango and ordered what a friend at home terms "the best Dessert Beer in the world today." Guinness Stout.

Sipping the blackish brew, feeling sorry for myself, I wondered how, of all people in the time-space continuum of one short dinner, I had begun to feel like the Second Coming of Dick Nixon.

Khai tapped me lightly on the shoulder.

"You watch CNN today?" he asked.

I nodded.

"Then you heard about the two boys who murdered their schoolmates and a teacher?" he asked gently.

I said, "Oh yeah."

Khai said, "Here in Vietnam we cannot imagine something like that happening. It was a shock, I could hardly move after I saw that story... I... just don't understand."

In Vietnam there was little violence on television, no guns

to speak of anywhere except in the military, little use of drugs, as well as firm family control of children.

I told him about the weapons that abounded in the U.S.A.

He wanted to know why that was.

"Our Constitution supports the right to bear arms."

Shaking his head, he asked, "Then why doesn't Congress amend the Constitution?"

I said, "It won't happen in my lifetime. Guns are to America, as Ho Chi Minh is to Vietnam."

I did not want to get into it because of my mixed feelings on the issue. I did not point out how the poorest people in rice paddies probably would have refused to have been bullied, enslaved, killed, and raped by tyrants over the many years if they had ever had the means to defend themselves. On the other hand, freedom to carry guns meant that morons, criminals, imbeciles, politicians, and even children would have access to them.

Gracefully Khai let me off the hook, nodding as if he understood.

I was sure that, coming from his context - No way.

When the bill was presented, Petite paid it in American dollars.

Khai bid farewell. We exchanged e-mail addresses.

The remainder of the crew decided to adjourn for a nightcap a few blocks away at *Lac Viet*.

It was an upstairs-downstairs cafe pub on the avenue skirting the eastern shore. The downstairs was crowded with tipsy foreigners. Huy led the way upstairs to an empty table.

I ordered a beer. The others opted for an upscale lemonade concoction.

Modern artwork on the walls, the place was tastefully decorated.

Huy asked me how I liked Hanoi.

I told him I thought it was the most beautiful city in Asia.

"Actually it's boring," he said. "I like Saigon. I think it's prettier and there's so much to do there. Many Northerners go south, but not many Southerners move up here."

I was now used to him disagreeing with every word I said and frankly I enjoyed it. Trying to steer the talk to a more positive course, I told him how much I liked the Ho Chi Minh Museum.

He said, "That was designed by foreigners."

I could tell that Auntie Giang, Petite, and Tu were enjoying each other's company by their brilliant smiles, laughter, and animated talk. We snapped several photographs.

I told Huy about our visit to the Temple of Literature, and pointed to the Vietnamese educational tradition, which I thought was somewhat unique in Asia.

He sipped his lemonade.

"Don't be fooled," he said. "As a whole society, Vietnamese don't really value education."

I countered, "It seems to me that there's an entire culture of learning. Academies dating from the earliest days. Mandarin exams from the tenth century. A long history."

He sighed heavily. "With few exceptions, Vietnam does not provide good education. America has no history to speak of, but it has the best university system in the world. History doesn't matter at all."

Spoken like a true engineer. I figured he had spent too much time calculating concrete stress factors; too little on why he was building dams in the first place.

I said, "Maybe it's unfair to compare Vietnam to America. As you say, we do have a wonderful university system. I think most countries would lack in comparison."

With a gloomy gaze, he said, "History is irrelevant. You

have just 200 years. That is nothing."

I said, "Really? Well, I don't agree. Time has speeded up, my friend, there's been more history made this century than in all the ones combined that came before. That is, history which produced great worldwide change."

Huy sipped his lemonade, not arguing the point.

I said, "I think what you mean is that if history mattered, then ancient countries such as Vietnam would have surpassed America. Perhaps in that respect, history *is* irrelevant."

He smiled. "I mean, we young people don't *care* about history. It's done with. We are looking forward. The past is done."

"What you really mean is: You want to *forget* the past."

"Not be burdened by it."

"Understandable," I said. "But you, Huy, are a product of the past. You want to build a dam, correct? That is because you want to control the uneven cycles of flooding and drought. History indicates that most years you have too much water, or too little. The dam should regulate the flow to provide a better life for the farmers."

It seemed we were both enjoying this *tete a tete*. Was I starting to sound like the Communist at the table?

With a hand motion and a nod, he conceded the point, then proceeded to another subject; something he considered so telling and irrefutable that I could scarcely argue.

He said, "Everything made here in Vietnam is fake. So-called 'Nike' shoes. 'Rolex' watches. Brand-name clothing you see on the street?" He waved his hands. "All fake. All crap."

The waiter hovered near our table, obviously eavesdropping. I ordered another round of drinks for the table. Our last night in Vietnam, and it had been the best conversation of the trip with the exception of Minh the River's input.

"Look, when I was a kid in the 1950s," I said, "the term

'Made in Japan' was a complete *joke*. It meant a product was 100 percent lousy. A total loser. But quality control is a learning process, and nothing more. Vietnam has tremendous resources, natural and otherwise. Your people are not only intelligent, they work hard. You give the country twenty years, and it can become another Taiwan."

He looked mortified.

"*Twenty* years? That's forever!"

I said, "Not in history, it isn't. That's nothing, remember? Do you agree that it's gotten much better economic-wise in the 1990s?"

Huy admitted it was true, even conceding that it was naive to think that economic success could happen overnight. It appeared that he was simply frustrated with the rate of progress.

Assuming the mantle of a Head Cheerleader, fortified with the righteous conviction of eight or nine beers, I placed a fatherly hand on his shoulder.

The waiter resumed his post, cocking an ear.

"Don't sell your country short. Don't sell yourself short," I said. "There are so many great things here you take for granted: Family values, warm generous people. Many such things. If you want to be negative, fine, but direct it toward something that makes a difference: Something like free education. Half the kids in Vietnam are cheated out of a chance for what you and I know as 'The Good Life.' People are bent over the fields out there earning 5,000 dong a day, who might even change the world if they had the advantages we had. I bet there's a million people in the paddies who are at least as smart as you or me."

Huy seemed to appreciate my little pep talk, if only because it showed I cared. Deliberately he shook his head.

I removed my hand and directed it to where it felt most comfortable.

Around a cold beer.

Huy laughed aloud.

"There aren't a million people *anywhere* as smart as you or me," he said.

I rolled my eyes. *Vietnamese stubbornness*!

The waiter smirked and walked away.

Contemporary newspaper pundits have pointed out that a great challenge for Vietnam's Communist Party will be to manage growing dissatisfaction among its original constituency, the peasantry, due to the widening disparity of income because of economic reform.

I came to the conclusion that it went further than that. Even those who had most benefited from either economic reform, or from their relationship with the regime, seemed dissatisfied.

I did not meet one person in Vietnam who volunteered a good thing to say about the government.

"TRIP OF A LIFETIME"

On Saturday morning I gobbled up a rich pair of breakfast eggs, knowing I would miss those.

The waitress placed a hand on Petite's shoulder, and said, "All the employees here at the restaurant have noticed how your Vietnamese has improved this week!"

It had never occurred to me that she did not speak the language perfectly. When I asked Petite about it, she said that over the years one lost fluency, due to forgetting words and the fact that the language itself was dynamic. She said that her thoughts were always in English. Her native tongue had long ago become a second language. Besides, she said, as a kid in Hue, she had tried to affect a northern accent. She liked the way it sounded more refined, so it was fun for her to finally get to practice her favorite dialect.

The background music in the restaurant was tuned low: "Making Friends" by Elton John. The day before, I had asked our recent acquaintance, the Aussie grande dame, to eighty-six "Funiculi Funiculae." The god-awful tune had been playing, it seemed endlessly, during every meal we ate in the hotel.

On cue with Elton John, the restaurant staff suddenly surrounded the table to say goodbye to Petite. It seemed they particularly enjoyed talking to *Viet Kieu*, whose experiences overseas in new lives were like dreams to them come back alive.

At one point, Petite asked the waitress if she had ever traveled out of the country.

"No," she giggled, "It is too expensive."

The good news was that anyone could get a passport. And the bad news: It cost $7,000. The average wage in the North was

$700-$800 per year. The Vietnamese business lady at Ha Long Bay had told us there were approximately 150 people in Hanoi who made as much as $500,000 per year; a handful relative to most large cities in the world today.

The waitress said she wasn't planning to go anywhere soon.

As we got up to leave, she thanked me for the recent demise of "Funiculi Funiculae." It was driving the employees crazy, too.

I remembered a muggy evening when I was eight years old. In a stuffy den without air-conditioning, they interrupted Howdy Doody to tell the television audience that Joseph Stalin had died. The way Stalin ran things, it was an evil empire. To a child, it was like the catharsis of the devil had passed away.

I thought of all that as we lined up and marched in two rows up a massive closed-off boulevard.

The Ho Chi Minh Mausoleum appeared ahead like a brick box next to the dreary sky. Again, foreigners were involved in this. The ambience was almost Eastern European, as the mausoleum was a replica of Lenin's Tomb in Moscow.

For awhile I goosestepped along as a Red Army soldier would at the Russian War Memorial in Berlin. The scene had Father Joe written all over it. May Day in March.

We halted at the entrance.

Petite asked a little girl in back of us if she knew who Bac Ho was. She didn't.

The person next to me was a young Vietnamese fellow, tour guide for two Scandinavian girls. He was also showing off and acting up in line. He told us that the local embalmers shipped the body back to Moscow for two months each autumn for refurbishing. He thought this was hilarious.

There were only six foreigners of about 300 people in line

for the tour, and we were all at the front. Gringo tickets cost more. No cameras were allowed inside, we had to check ours at the ticket booth. As the line moved again, we filed past an honor guard.

Inside, we walked slowly around a pathway surrounding the body. The dark room and spotlights in the middle would not have done much for anyone's complexion.

The face and hands looked waxy. Madame Tussaud's in London was better at that sort of thing.

The irony was that Ho, if he had had a say in the matter, would not have been caught dead in a place like the Ho Chi Minh Mausoleum.

In Ha Long Bay, the Norwegians told us that they had visited Ho Chi Minh's home. They marveled at how simple and charming, and how "efficient" it was. The clothes that covered his body in the mausoleum were the dark peasant costume he often wore. What GIs called "pajamas."

At some time before his death in 1969, Ho sat down and wrote out a Last Will and Testament. In this, he stated that he wished to be cremated, and that his ashes be placed in urns atop three specific hilltops. Also, he had several naive comments in the document about returning the state's power to the people.

So I felt sorry for Bac Ho.

Lenin, Stalin, and Mao were natural born killers that even Hollywood could not dream up because they would come off as too "unrealistic."

Vietnam was not a dangerous place, but it had its share of scam artists. At the front desk, checking out, the clerk insisted that the hotel collect the money for the taxi ride to the airport. It was better, she told us, that we not owe the driver anything. He would collect his fare after delivery.

Our favorite doorman opened the door with a flourish and a

big smile.

I had given him a larger tip than usual for raving against the Commies out on the street and providing material for this book.

Several months before the trip while visiting friends in Corpus Christi, it happened after a dinner given for Gatemouth Brown, one of the world's special musicians and a legend in his own mind.

Gate and Larry and Jen had gone on to *Doctor Rockit's*, the blues bar, to set up for the show.

Jimmy was left sitting across from me.

He was a world-class sailor and had taken many a journey that you and I only dream about, unless you've also hunted lobsters off an uninhabited island in the Bahamas. After tequila, I was telling him about the forthcoming trip to Vietnam.

He raised off the chair.

"God, Truman," he said. "That's a *Trip of a Lifetime*."

And that was surely what I was expecting it to be, Jimmy just put the words to it.

In retrospect, Vietnam in 1998 was a place where it was thrilling to be dazzled by the sensory overload. The streets seemed so empty when we got back to the United States. I have searched for an adjective that might convey in a single word the overall impact. The best I could come up with was: Amazing.

Vietnam was not a vacation. It was traveling a black ribbon road through green rice fields. It was talking to people. It was a learning process. It was a hell of a fine impression. One could easily see a Vietnam that was more bizarre, or more native, or less expensive than the one we saw.

Before the trip, I thought of it as a country that I would not wish to go to more than once. But Vietnam became one of my favorite places on earth, a place that produced emotional reaction from almost everyone who had ever been there.

Each journey back would be another "Trip of a Lifetime."
"Petite! When's the next plane for Saigon?"